Florida Lighthouses

Florida Lighthouses

Text by
Kevin M. McCarthy

Paintings by
William L. Trotter

Maps by
Marjorie A. Niblack

University of Florida Press
Gainesville

Copyright © 1990 by the Board of Regents of the State of Florida
All rights reserved
Printed in the U.S.A. on acid-free paper

04 03 02 01 00 99   P   8   7   6   5   4

99 98 97 96 95 94   93   C   8   7   6   5   4   3   2

Library of Congress Cataloging-in-Publication Data
McCarthy, Kevin.
p. cm.
ISBN 0-8130-0982-0 (alk. paper). — ISBN 0-8130-0993-6 (pbk.:
alk. paper)
1. Lighthouses—Florida—Guide—books 2. Florida–Description and
travel—1981– —Guide-books. I. Trotter, William L. II. Title.
VKIO24.F6M33 1990
387.1'5–dc20   89-29035 CIP

Florida lighthouses / text by Kevin M. McCarthy; paintings by
William L. Trotter; maps by Marjorie A. Niblack.

The University Press of Florida is the scholarly publishing agency for
the State University System of Florida, comprising Florida A & M
University, Florida Atlantic University, Florida International University, Florida State University, University of Central Florida, University
of Florida, University of North Florida, University of South Florida,
and University of West Florida.

University Press of Florida
15 Northwest 15th Street
Gainesville, FL 32611
http://www.upf.com

Contents

Florida Lighthouses (map) vi–vii
Introduction 1
  1. Amelia Island Lighthouse 5
  2. St. Johns River Lighthouse 9
  3. St. Johns Lightship 13
  4. St. Johns Light Station 17
  5. St. Augustine Lighthouse 21
  6. Ponce de Leon Inlet Lighthouse 25
  7. Cape Canaveral Lighthouse 29
  8. Jupiter Inlet Lighthouse 33
  9. Hillsboro Inlet Lighthouse 37
10. Cape Florida Lighthouse 41
11. Fowey Rocks Lighthouse 45
12. Carysfort Reef Lighthouse 49
13. Alligator Reef Lighthouse 53
14. Sombrero Key Lighthouse 57
15. American Shoal Lighthouse 61
16. Sand Key Lighthouse 65
17. Key West Lighthouse 69
18. Garden Key Lighthouse 73
19. Dry Tortugas Lighthouse 77
20. Sanibel Island Lighthouse 81
21. Port Boca Grande Lighthouse 85
22. Boca Grande Lighthouse (Entrance Range Rear) 89
23. Egmont Key Lighthouse 93
24. Anclote Key Lighthouse 97
25. Seahorse Key Lighthouse 101
26. St. Marks Lighthouse 105
27. Crooked River Lighthouse 109
28. Cape St. George Lighthouse 113
29. Cape San Blas Lighthouse 117
30. St. Joseph Bay Lighthouse 121
31. Pensacola Lighthouse 125
Index 129

FLORIDA LIGHTHOUSES

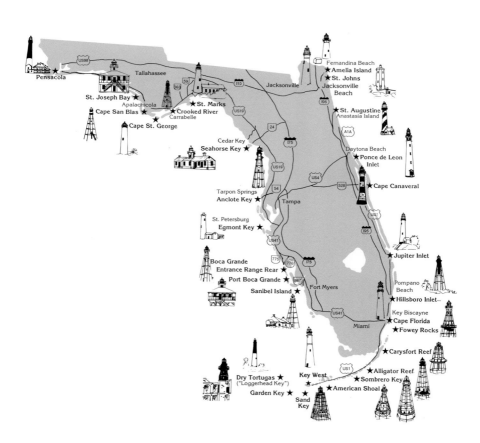

Pensacola

US98

Tallahassee

St. Joseph Bay ★
Apalachicola
Cape San Blas ★
★ Crooked River
Cape St. George ★
Carrabelle
★ St. Marks

59
163

112

24

I75

US19

US19

Jacksonville

Fernandina Beach
★ Amelia Island
★ St. Johns
Jacksonville
Beach

★ St. Augustine
Anastasia Island

A1A

Daytona Beach
★ Ponce de Leon
Inlet

★ Cape Canaveral

Cedar Key
★ Seahorse Key

Tarpon Springs
Anclote Key ★

I95

528

US4

54

Tampa

St. Petersburg
Egmont Key ★

US41

Boca Grande
Entrance Range Rear ★
Port Boca Grande ★
Sanibel Island ★

775 726

I75

867

Fort Myers

US41

Miami

US1

I95

★ Jupiter Inlet

Pompano
Beach

★ Hillsboro Inlet

Key Biscayne
★ Cape Florida
★ Fowey Rocks

★ Carysfort Reef

Dry Tortugas ★
("Loggerhead Key")
Garden Key ★

Key West

US1

Sand
Key

★ Alligator Reef
★ Sombrero Key
★ American Shoal

Florida is a peninsula that rose out of the sea eons ago and has depended on the sea for its fishing, commerce, tourism, and very identity. In the state's 1,000-plus miles of coastline one can find beaches for vacationers, inlets and rivers for fishermen, even a launching pad for rockets, but that coastline also holds dangers for the unwary.

Two centuries ago pirates could dart out from the many uncharted inlets to wreak havoc on defenseless ships. One hundred fifty years ago Indians massacred white settlers along the eastern coast in their last desperate attempt to drive them out and keep the land for themselves. One hundred years ago ship salvagers, the infamous wreckers in the Florida Keys, preyed on ships in distress, sometimes luring them onto the deadly offshore reef by displaying false lights on the beach.

Worse than the pirates, Indians, and wreckers are the gales and hurricanes that have buffeted the Florida coast. In the last 400 years fierce storms have beached or sunk countless ships, from Spanish treasure galleons to luxury liners, from rum-runners to submarines. Even today treasure hunters with metal detectors scouring beaches after a storm may find Spanish doubloons and jewelry from ages past.

Two great ocean currents flow in opposite directions off Florida's east coast. The Gulf Stream, bright blue in color and warmer than the surrounding Atlantic, flows north from the Gulf of Mexico, eventually reaching Europe some 5,000 miles to the far northeast. The colder Labrador Current flows south, closer to shore, pushing southbound ships on their way. What lies beneath that calm sea, namely the Florida Reef, has torn out the bottom of many an unsuspecting ship that wandered onto it, with great loss of life and cargo. The Gulf of Mexico off the west coast also has dangers in the form of sandbars, oyster beds, and mud flats, all waiting to catch a ship unawares.

Introduction

To protect ships from the many hazards along the Florida coast and to provide mariners a bearing, the federal government began erecting lighthouses in the 1820s, giving each structure a distinctive color for daytime reckoning and a unique light sequence for nighttime identification. Florida presented new problems to engineers assigned to build lighthouses along its coast, for they found that they could not simply continue building the traditional New England brick tower. For one thing, Florida's soft coastal sand could not support the great weight of the large brick structures common in Maine and Massachusetts. Engineers had to come up with a new type of foundation (to be explained later), especially in the Florida Keys, where waves washed over the sandbars around the lighthouses, making islands appear, disappear, and reappear over time.

Lighthouse builders and keepers also had to contend with human conflicts on land. In the mid-1800s, Seminole Indians harassed builders, killed one keeper, and tried to burn Cape Florida Lighthouse to the ground. During the Civil War, local southern sympathizers extinguished the lights of the lighthouses so that blockade-runners could move contraband under cover of darkness inland and ashore, but the lack of lights caused much consternation among ordinary sailors looking for familiar landmarks. During World War II, lighthouse keepers faced the dilemma of whether to light their lamps at night for the many Allied ships along the coast, knowing that the light would also provide a clearer view for Nazi submarines lurking nearby with their torpedoes.

The fascinating story of the Florida lighthouse is one of great engineering accomplishments and lonely service along isolated coasts. The silent sentinels that remain in the state bear testimony to a job well done. How long they will endure depends to a great extent on their local communities and the some quarter of a million annual visitors to the towers still standing. The state's thirty lighthouses and one lightship are, for the most part, still sending their beams out across the sea at night and offering a welcome sight to the weary navigator.

Operation of the lighthouses has changed hands over the years. On 7 August 1789, the U.S. Congress passed an act empowering the Treasury Department to assume responsibility for all aids to navigation and lighthouses in our newly independent country. In 1820, the fifth auditor of the treasury took charge of the aids to navigation and became popularly known as the general superintendent of lighthouses. In 1852, Congress created the nine-

Introduction

member Lighthouse Board, an efficient group of dedicated officials who dramatically improved aids to navigation in the United States. In 1910, Congress established the Bureau of Lighthouses in the Commerce Department, streamlining the operation, putting one man in charge, and decreasing the military presence in the lighthouse service. In 1939, the U.S. Coast Guard took over operation of the lighthouses in this country and began an efficient maintenance program that continues to this day.

Having lived ten summers of my youth near Barnegat Lighthouse in New Jersey, I have always been intrigued by lighthouses; in 1986 I began to visit as many of the Florida structures as were accessible. I also examined the records from the National Archives concerning lighthouses; pored over century-old logbooks on microfilm; found and interviewed in Port St. Joe, Florida, the son of a lighthouse keeper; and visited libraries and museums throughout the state gathering material.

Bill Trotter, the artist whose paintings are reproduced in this book, showed me through his Lighthouse Museum in Jacksonville Beach, Florida, and agreed to collaborate in putting this book together. It differs from similar books on the subject in that it uses paintings instead of photographs of the lighthouses, paintings that picture the structures in their prime, basically around the turn of this century. It also uses archival material from Washington and Tallahassee, as well as the records maintained by the keepers over the years. I have spent much time in the past two years climbing around and up lighthouses, including one in which the Coast Guardsman would not allow my eight-months' pregnant wife to go to the top, having visions of her giving birth at the top of the tower.

This book is dedicated to all those keepers, both men and women, who have maintained the state's coastal beacons through storms and fog and who have therefore made the sea a safer place.

1

Amelia Island Lighthouse

High above Egan's Creek on the lovely island of Amelia is the first Florida lighthouse one meets heading south from Georgia. The short white tower marks the mouth of the St. Marys River and the approach to Nassau Sound. Amelia Island, part of the Sea Island chain that begins in North Carolina and ends in north Florida, is similar in size to New York's populous Manhattan Island, but it has only about 10,000 inhabitants. It lies peacefully between the Atlantic Ocean on the east and some 4,000 acres of tidal marsh on the west and between the busy ports of Savannah to the north and Jacksonville to the south.

At several points in history Amelia Island and its chief town, Fernandina Beach, were on the brink of big development, but neither ever lived up to the grandiose plans of their early settlers, partly because of a yellow fever outbreak, the rise of Jacksonville to the south, and the migration of many of their people to better jobs elsewhere. Although fewer and fewer ships continued to use the port there, authorities early on realized the necessity of a lighthouse for the many ships that passed offshore.

In 1839, the federal government built a lighthouse on Amelia Island, a red-brick conical tower painted white. The importance of the lighthouse increased during the 1850s when workers built Florida's first cross-state railroad from Fernandina Beach to Cedar Key. During the years leading up to the Civil War, Amelia Island became quite busy as ships used its port for the loading and unloading of lumber and military equipment. After the war, with the Fernandina Beach–Cedar Key railroad line destroyed, the Amelia Island port attracted fewer ships, and the area settled into a quieter existence.

From the sea during the daytime one can just make out the top of the lighthouse nestled among the trees and overlooking a tidal marsh. Situated more inland and on higher ground than most Florida lighthouses, the 64-foot tower stands 107 feet above

Amelia Island Lighthouse

sea level and sends out a light every ten seconds that sailors 23 miles from land can see. The promontory on which the lighthouse rests is unusual topography along the Florida coast since most of the lighthouses lie close to the ocean on flat land, often washed by high tides and subject to dangerous erosion. The hillside location necessitates a shorter tower than elsewhere along the coast since there is a certain optimal height for the placement of a fire or light to be seen far at sea. If the light is too high, mist and fog hide it, making it useless to sailors. If the light is too low, sand dunes or trees block its range.

In a town well known for its restored nineteenth-century historic homes, the stark lines of the Amelia Island Lighthouse remind one that engineers designed such buildings to be simple, practical, and easily maintained. The circular brick wall is four feet thick at the base and tapers as it rises. One can still see cracks in the tower wall caused when a fierce hurricane tilted the building precariously; engineers somehow jacked the tower back up with no serious damage to the structure. The winding granite steps leading to the top of the tower were hand hewn in New England and brought by ship to Fernandina Beach.

Amelia Island Lighthouse

The light itself consists of hundreds of prisms, each one numbered for ease of replacement. The name of French light-maker Barbier Bernard appears, but without a date. In the early days before modernization, the lighthouse keeper had to light the light each evening and extinguish it each morning. For fuel he used whale oil at first, then kerosene, and finally electricity. He also had to wind up the heavy cables that powered the rotating mechanism and clean and polish the light thoroughly each day.

Because Amelia Island Lighthouse was smaller than other Florida lights, the keeper there did not usually have an assistant, and so a disabling accident to the keeper necessitated that his wife work the light. In 1881, for example, when the keeper mashed his big toe, his wife took over the duties until he recovered. That was typical of the way lighthouse families pitched in and helped each other in, up, and around the tower. Another trait among keepers was the continuity of service. Before the Coast Guard took over the lighthouse service, the last civilian keeper was Thomas J. O'Hagan. Himself the son of a lighthouse keeper at Amelia, he married a direct descendant of the first keeper, Amos Latham.

As at other lighthouses the keeper kept a logbook to record the daily weather conditions, including occasional frost and ice, and anything out of the ordinary. One night, for example, a duck flew into the storm pane and broke it. In another entry, the keeper, Mr. Sydam, noted the day that he had stopped using tobacco.

In 1891, when he turned sixty-three and retired from his duties, Mr. Sydam noted in the logbook: "20 years ago I commenced in the Light House Service; have been absent but one night during the time." He was just one of a string of men who served on Amelia Island and helped maintain the lighthouse on one of the more isolated, undramatic Florida sites.

How to get to the lighthouse

From I-95 heading south take the second exit below the Georgia state line (No. 129) onto U.S. A1A east into Amelia Island, taking a right turn onto Atlantic Avenue, which is still U.S. A1A. One mile farther on, turn left on N. 20th Street, go to the stop sign, turn right on Highland Street, and immediately turn left on Lighthouse Circle, then follow the road around. The lighthouse is on the left at the top of the road.

Florida Lighthouses

  From the beach follow U.S. A1A to N. 20th Street and follow the above instructions.

  Permission from the Coast Guard is needed to enter the grounds, but the tower can still be seen from various points in the area.

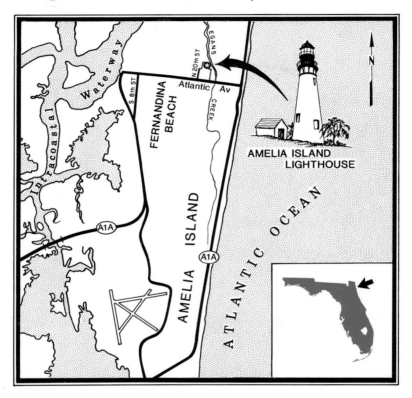

AMELIA ISLAND LIGHTHOUSE

2

St. Johns River Lighthouse

The St. Johns River enters the Atlantic Ocean at Mayport near the place where French explorer Jean Ribault first established a settlement in 1565. The Intracoastal Waterway a little to the west adds to the boat traffic, as do ships from the Mayport Naval Air Station and local fishermen entering and leaving the harbor. Hundreds of large freighters serving Jacksonville and north Florida use the river, making it one of the most commercial in the state.

Because the river's currents at the mouth meet the ocean in such a striking way, the early Spanish explorers called it Río de Corrientes, River of Currents. Its present name came from a 1590 mission established near the mouth of the river, the Mission San Juan del Puerto, St. John of the Harbor; this was shortened to San Juan and then Anglicized to St. John's and then St. Johns.

Northeasters and other strong winds used to play havoc with the channel at the mouth of the river, especially before engineers built jetties to try to stabilize conditions. Civic-minded people who wanted to make Jacksonville a first-class port able to handle large ships argued long and hard throughout the nineteenth century for deepening the St. Johns. Before the dredging of the harbor, engineers realized the necessity of marking the bar for ships and building jetties. Since that time workers have continued improving the situation, especially when construction of the Naval Air Station added aircraft carriers and many other vessels to the channels.

Congress began appropriating money to build a lighthouse at the mouth of the St. Johns in 1828 in what was then the Territory of Florida, 17 years before Florida became a state. Engineers built the first tower in 1830 near the present south jetty. When the encroaching ocean weakened that first lighthouse, workers tore it down and built a second one in 1835 about a mile up the river. In time, shifting sands and the strong river current threatened to undermine that structure, and sand dunes around the keeper's house blocked the light for ships approaching the coastline.

9

St. Johns River Lighthouse

The federal government refused to fix the lighthouse because its site did not belong to the government and because the hollowness of the tower's walls made the raising of the building dubious.

In 1859, after doing another survey of the area, engineers built the present lighthouse across the bar from the old structure. When the Civil War began, Yankee gunboats used the lighthouse for guidance in the changing, narrow channel of the St. Johns River until a Confederate sympathizer shot out the tower's light. During the rest of the war, mariners had to rely on lanterns in the area, a chancy measure that put their ships at risk. After the war, engineers repaired the light and, in 1887, raised the tower fifteen feet to its present height.

The year 1889 almost saw the end of the 81-foot lighthouse there when surveyors recommended that it be replaced by a first-order, 150-foot lighthouse on Fort George Island to the north; a first-order structure was the most powerful one and referred to the structure of the lens and lamp. Proponents of the new lighthouse pointed out that it could replace the St. Johns Lighthouse and even the Amelia Island Lighthouse since its powerful, first-order lens would reach the area to the north covered by the lighthouse at

St. Johns River Lighthouse

Little Cumberland Island, Georgia, and the area to the south covered by the St. Augustine Lighthouse. It would have been second in power on the Atlantic coast to the lighthouse at the Highlands of Navesink, New Jersey. Nothing happened because Congress failed to act on the recommendation.

In 1929, a lightship off Mayport in the Atlantic Ocean replaced the St. Johns Lighthouse, and, in 1954, a modern beacon light on the eastern edge of the naval station replaced the lightship. In the 1950s, the navy talked about razing the old lighthouse to eliminate what it called a minor hazard to its airplanes, but angry neighbors successfully prevented it. Some area residents feel that the lighthouse makes aircraft fly higher than they might otherwise do and thus lessens the noise at the busy military airport. In 1969, the Coast Guard turned over the old lighthouse to the navy, which bought 350 surrounding acres for the Mayport Naval Station. The navy did some restoration work on the tower in a good-will move, and in 1982 officials placed it on the National Register of Historic Places.

Today the red-brick tower that area people call the Mayport Lighthouse offers quite a contrast to the advanced technology of the surrounding naval station, but it offers a welcome sight to the many fishing boats, yachts, and naval vessels going into and out of Mayport. Because the tower stands innocuously in a remote corner of the naval station, it may eventually become part of a public park/museum complex. That would enable visitors to get a better feel for what life was like in one of the earliest parts of nineteenth-century Florida.

How to get to the lighthouse

Take U.S. A1A to Mayport and turn left into the U.S. Naval Station. Auto registration, driver's license, and proof of insurance must be presented at the visitors' building in order to get onto the base during the naval station's open house hours on weekends. The lighthouse stands at the northwest corner of the naval station. The old brick tower can be seen by driving a quarter mile east of the ferry that crosses the St. Johns.

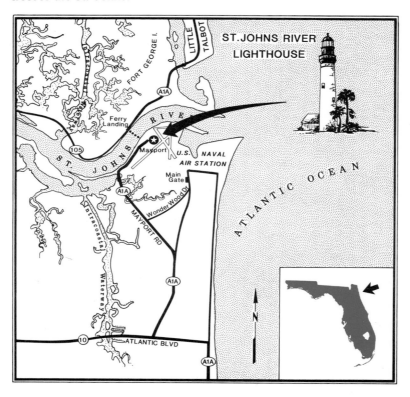

3

St. Johns Lightship

When mariners complained about the inadequacy of the St. Johns River Lighthouse in the nineteenth century, those interested in developing the port of Jacksonville urged authorities to place a lightship several miles out at sea from the mouth of the river. Editorialists argued that a lightship with a double set of lamps, a loud foghorn, and a tolling bell could better guide ships into port, especially during the dreaded fogs that shrouded the area, whereas ships would have to approach dangerously near to the coastline to see a lighthouse and might never see it during a thick fog. Proponents of the lightship pointed out that nearby cities like Brunswick, Savannah, and Charleston all had lightships and lighthouses and were prospering commercially.

Lightships had a long history of helping navigators find their way past treacherous shores. Historians have traced the ancestor of the lightship to the Romans several centuries before the birth of Christ. Roman galleys patrolling the coast had lighted fire baskets on the masthead to show both merchants and pirates that the ships were there to help commerce. A closer prototype of the modern lightship was an eighteenth-century British ship that suspended two lanterns from a crossarm as an aid to ships sailing the Thames River at night.

Lightships proved to be quite useful in the nineteenth century, although the number varied depending on whether they were in favor. In 1837, 26 such vessels served in this country; by 1852, the number had increased to 42, but it dropped to 33 by 1893: 28 on the Atlantic coast, four on lakes, and one on the Pacific coast. By 1917, the number increased to 53 lightship stations. In this century the numbers steadily declined in the last sixty years:

13

Florida Lighthouses

Year	Number of lightships in service
1920	49
1930	44
1940	25
1950	28
1960	24
1970	9
1985	0

In the nineteenth century money was so scarce for lightships that no relief ships replaced those that had to leave for repairs. A station could be without any lightship for months while the vessel assigned there was in dry dock. Such vessels also could not afford to carry spare parts so that, if some important piece of machinery malfunctioned, the ship had to return to port for a replacement.

Lighthouse authorities who opposed placing a lightship near Mayport pointed out that a modern lightship for the St. Johns River would cost $300,000, with an annual maintenance of $60,000. Proponents of the lightship pointed out that the value of the vessel over a lighthouse at the mouth of the St. Johns lay in the fact that the former allowed a ship to establish its position five miles off the river entrance, which could be important during fog or a storm.

While interested parties argued for and against a lightship, the forces of nature helped decide the issue. When fog stranded the Clyde Liner *Lake Elsmere* off the St. Johns Bar in 1922, the Jacksonville Board of Trade adopted as its slogan "Get a lightship for Jacksonville." Several months later the *Lenape* with 227 passengers aboard ran aground at the mouth of the river in a heavy fog. It was time for action, but it still took another seven years before authorities moved the lightship *Brunswick* from Brunswick, Georgia, to a site off the St. Johns. In 1929, they renamed the ship *St. Johns* and used it to replace the lighthouse there. Anchored about seven miles offshore in 57 feet of water, the lightship guided ships into the mouth of the St. Johns with a 13,000-candlepower electric light visible 14 miles away. A foghorn, radio beacon, and distance-finding station completed its equipment.

St. Johns Lightship

Once the Coast Guard took over lighthouses and lightships on 1 July 1939, the men stationed on the lightship liked the 20 percent sea duty pay they received on top of their regular pay and also the eight-day leave they received every 20 days, but they did not like the danger and the seasickness and the loneliness associated with the ships. Living with eight or nine men in a confined ship and having only an occasional fisherman or yachtsman visit them made a monotonous routine. Whenever the ship was in port for repairs, Lightship 109, named *Relief,* took over the station.

The lightship off Mayport served a useful purpose as an aid to navigation, but it had its share of problems. In 1947, for example, storms blew it off station twice, and it took several hours for it to resume its position, a time that might have caused ships in the area serious problems. There was always the danger of collision, as happened elsewhere when large ships collided with lightships, always at the peril of the latter. Finally, the expense of keeping a lightship off Mayport, the danger and isolation for the men assigned there, and the improved technological advances for land-based lighthouses made its replacement mandatory. In 1954, a modern beacon light on the eastern edge of the naval station replaced the lightship, providing a modern, safer, technologically superior light.

How to get to the lightship

The lightship has not been in the area for many years, but it may be moved back to Jacksonville as a museum.

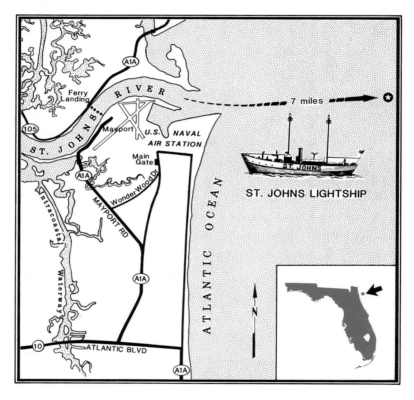

ST. JOHNS LIGHTSHIP

4

St. Johns Light Station

A newer, modern-looking, 64-foot, concrete lighthouse, called the St. Johns Light Station, replaced the St. Johns River Lightship in 1954. Its aero-marine beacon has a white light of 200,000 candlepower that can guide ships that are 22 nautical miles out at sea and has a fog signal at the end of the jetties. The light station has been completely automated since 1967 so that an alarm system at the station alerts the Coast Guard station in case of a malfunction.

This particular structure represents one of several kinds of lighthouse along Florida's coastline. Engineers designed the different structures to fit the needs of a particular site, from the large masonry towers of Ponce de Leon Inlet, St. Marks, and Pensacola, to the screw-pile lighthouses along the Florida Keys, to the spindly towers of Sanibel, Crooked River, and Cape San Blas. The St. Johns Light Station resembles the automated light on Egmont Key near St. Petersburg in its modernity and nontraditional top.

The light at the top of the St. Johns Light Station represented a development from the old lights. The first lighthouses used fires on top of towers to warn ships at sea of the reef or an inlet. Early lighthouse keepers were called wick-trimmers or wickies from their daily practice of trimming from the old asbestos or flax wicks in the lamps the residue of the previous night's burning. In order to concentrate the light into one powerful beam, engineers used various reflecting systems, especially the type that French physicist Augustin Fresnel designed in 1822, which used prisms and magnifying bull's-eyes to concentrate the beams of light into a single, sharp beam as the lens revolved around it. The beehive-shaped lens around a single lamp came in seven sizes or orders, beginning with a first order, the most powerful and one used in the more important lighthouses.

The manning of the St. Johns Light Station by the Coast Guard represented a late development of lighthouses in the

St. Johns Light Station

United States. After the American Revolution the federal government assumed responsibility for building and maintaining lighthouses in the United States. Since then, different governmental bodies have been in charge of lighthouses until the Coast Guard assumed responsibility for manning and maintaining the structures.

The building of the St. Johns Light Station, which looks so different from the massive towers of New England, may have disappointed some of the more nostalgic public, but it serves its function well of alerting offshore ships as to where they are. Up until the middle of the twentieth century lighthouses needed the reliable services of the keepers because the equipment was liable to fail at crucial times, as during a gale. After assuming control of American lighthouses in 1939, the Coast Guard began to use battery power for the smaller lights. Later, the development of transistors and solid-state circuits allowed the Coast Guard to standardize and upgrade the equipment that monitors lighthouse operations, and under its Lighthouse Automation and Modernization Program (LAMP) the Coast Guard has automated most of the lights in the United States. It costs about $100,000 to automate a station, but salaries saved pay for the conversion in about four years. Today the National Weather Service uses lighthouses to monitor weather and sea conditions.

Before the establishment of the St. Johns Light Station in 1954, the area along the beach south of there was so deserted that during World War II a German submarine dropped off four would-be saboteurs near Jacksonville Beach. The men went ashore in June 1942, made their way to Jacksonville, and headed north with the plan of meeting up with four German spies who had landed on Long Island. The FBI eventually arrested all the spies, six of whom were executed. The fact that four of them could land undetected near Jacksonville Beach pointed out the need for more patrolling on the beaches during wartime and showed how isolated the area was.

If the powerful beacon on top of the St. Johns Light Station disappoints the lighthouse aficionado accustomed to the traditional masonry tower, the mariner at sea is glad for its strong illumination and not at all interested in the beauty of the structure itself. That tower represents a new type of lighthouse: sleek, functional, practical. From a landlubber's point of view, the old conical structures with their lanterns housed at the top and the long spiral staircase leading to a narrow parapet were monolithic towers of beauty. From the mariner's point of view the new structures are just as good because of their dependability and accuracy.

How to get to the light station

As for the St. Johns Lighthouse, check at the gate to the Mayport Naval Station on weekends when the base has open hours. Then proceed north on Maine Sreet, east on Moale Avenue, and one block north on Baltimore Street. The lighthouse is off to the east near the ocean.

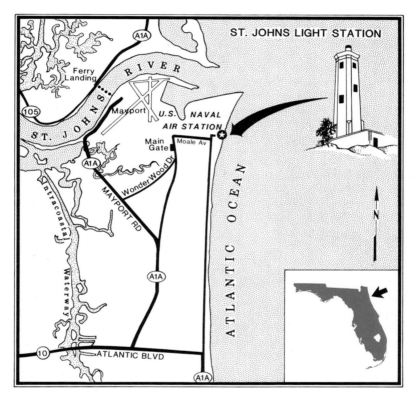

5

St. Augustine Lighthouse

The stately, striped lighthouse on Anastasia Island at the entrance to St. Augustine's inlet in northeastern Florida is probably the most visually striking of Florida's lighthouses. Like the Cape Hatteras Lighthouse in North Carolina, the Anastasia Island tower's black-and-white helixes resemble a huge barberpole, clearly different from the solid towers in Amelia Island and Mayport to the north and Ponce de Leon Inlet to the south.

An early Anastasia Island lookout tower, which the Spanish used in the sixteenth century to warn the settlers about impending danger, attracted the English sailor Sir Francis Drake, who was heading north along the Florida coast in May 1586. While investigating the tower more closely, Drake's forces discovered the Spanish town on the mainland and burned it down. Almost 200 years later, during the time that England controlled Florida (1763–83), the English built a tower on the same spot as the lookout tower and put a cannon at the top. Sentries fired the cannon to signal the town that a ship was approaching and hoisted flags at the north or south end to tell the townspeople which direction the ship was coming from. At night the sentries tended a large fire to guide vessels along the coast.

Spain regained the territory of Florida from England in 1783 but finally ceded it to the United States in 1821. Stephen Pleasonton, the man in charge of constructing and maintaining lighthouses throughout the United States at that time, built a lighthouse on Anastasia in 1824, with the oil lamp some 73 feet above sea level and visible for 14 miles. John Andreu was appointed lighthouse keeper there for an annual salary of $350. Andreu was a pilot from St. Augustine and therefore was acquainted with the difficulty of entering and leaving the port there.

At the start of the Civil War, Confederate sympathizers put out the light, and it remained out of commission until 1867. As the sea crept closer and closer to the structure, eroding much land around the tower, authorities obtained five acres of land about

St. Augustine Lighthouse

a half-mile from the old tower and began constructing a new one around 1871. The ocean continued eroding land on the island, eventually reaching within ten feet of the rising brick-and-iron tower. Northeasters caused much more beach erosion there than did hurricanes, primarily because hurricane-generated winds and waves, while severe, are short lived and localized, whereas a northeast storm may generate strong winds and waves over a larger area for a longer time.

Engineers hurriedly began mining a nearby quarry for soft limestone called coquina, a sedimentary material composed of shell fragments and coral that had been used in the construction of

St. Augustine Lighthouse

St. Augustine's formidable Castillo de San Marcos. Workers constructed a jetty of coquina and brush in time to hold back the ocean and finished building the lighthouse.

After workers installed a first-order Fresnel lens in the tower, a light strong enough to be seen for 19 miles, the keeper lighted it on 15 October 1874. In addition to the 19-mile fixed light, a second light flashing once every 30 seconds was visible for 24 miles. The old 1824 tower finally toppled into the sea in 1880.

The original lard oil lamps in the tower gave way to wick-burning kerosene lamps of 13,000 candlepower and, finally, an electric bulb of 1,000 watts that can generate a beam of 20,000 candlepower. During the early days, the keeper had to carry three gallons of kerosene up the 227 steps to the lantern room and light the lamp at dusk. In the morning, he had to lower the curtains to shut out the sun's rays. When engineers electrified the tower in 1936, the keeper could light the lamp by turning on a switch at the base of the tower, although he still had to raise and lower the curtain to protect the lens from the sun.

While the logbook faithfully kept by the men on duty seldom varied from a routine notation of the weather and the infrequent visitor, occasionally something unusual happened. On the night of 31 August 1886, the keeper noted: "An Earthquake passed through the Station at 9:20 P.M. The tower swayed in a violent manner. No damage was done to the Station." One doesn't usually think of Florida as having earthquakes, but they did occur.

Several authors wrote about the St. Augustine Lighthouse, including Constance Fenimore Woolson (1840–94), grand-niece of American novelist James Fenimore Cooper and a novelist/ poet who lived in St. Augustine and wrote about Florida. One of her poems, "The Florida Beach," contained the following stanza about a lighthouse that resembled the one on Anastasia Island:

> The Spanish light-house stands in haze:
> 　　The keeper trims his light;
> No sail he sees through the long, long days,
> 　　No sail through the still, still night.
> But ships that pass far out to sea,
> 　　Along the warm Gulf Stream,
> From Cuba and the tropic Carribee,
> 　　Keep watch for his distant gleam.

That distant gleam was reduced in power during World War II from 20,000 to 5,000 candlepower in order to make it more difficult for enemy submarines to spot the ships that passed near the light and torpedo them. In 1970, fire damaged the keepers' quarters, but workers restored them and converted them into a museum in 1988. Today the lighthouse has an automatic light that flashes through the night every thirty seconds, continuing to guide mariners as it has for more than 100 years.

How to get to the lighthouse

From St. Augustine cross the Bridge of Lions to Anastasia Island. One mile from the bridge, turn left off route U.S. A1A to Busam Street and then right on Lighthouse Avenue. The museum, housed in the two-storied lighthouse keepers' house, has exhibits, a period room, and a video theater. Open during daylight hours. Phone: 904-829-0745. Admission fee.

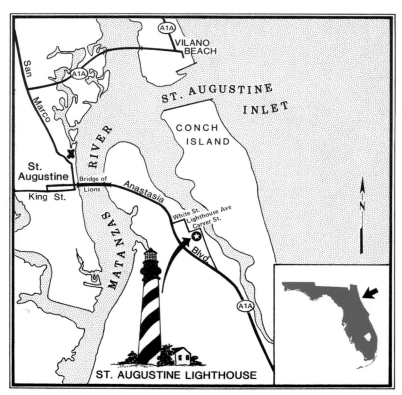

ST. AUGUSTINE LIGHTHOUSE

6

Ponce de Leon Inlet Lighthouse

"None of them knew the color of the sky." Thus begins one of America's most famous short stories, "The Open Boat," by Stephen Crane. The story took place off the coast near Daytona Beach, as did the actual shipwreck that Crane experienced in 1897. Crane was on his way to cover the Cuban Revolution for his newspaper when his ship, the *Commodore*, began taking on water and quickly sank. The famous writer, best known for *The Red Badge of Courage*, struggled into a dinghy with several seamen from the ship and, with much difficulty, eventually made the shore, after which he wrote up his experiences. In that story, the ship's survivors caught sight of what was then called the Mosquito Inlet Lighthouse and steered toward it, hoping the lighthouse keeper would see them and send a rescue team. To them, the lighthouse represented the possibility of a quick rescue and the safety of shore.

That lighthouse took its name from the nearby inlet and the fact that the Spanish had called the land there Los Mosquitos. The name "Mosquito" was an accurate reminder of how prevalent the pesky bugs were in former days and how annoying such pests could be for lighthouse families living near swamps and lakes. Chambers of Commerce have managed to euphemize many such names since that time, for example changing Mosquito County to Orange County and Mosquito River in Volusia County to Halifax River. In 1926, Mosquito Inlet became Ponce de Leon Inlet, honoring the Spanish explorer who discovered Florida in 1513.

Ponce de Leon Inlet, joining the Halifax River to the north and Indian River North to the south, provided challenges to mariners passing through the narrow channel and crossing the shallow bar on their way to the harbor at New Smyrna. The wrecks occurring there and along the beach pointed up the necessity for a lighthouse. During the British control of Florida, local authorities maintained a blockhouse and a beacon at the inlet with skilled pilots to

Ponce de Leon Inlet Lighthouse

help ships steer over the dangerous bar. In 1830, local planters and ship captains petitioned Congress for a lighthouse, with the result that engineers drew up plans for such a structure.

In 1835, a well-known builder of the day, Winslow Lewis of Boston, constructed a lighthouse and nearby dwelling on the south side of the inlet for about $7,500. Even after William H. Williams became the lighthouse keeper at an annual salary of $450, officials could not light the lamp because they never received the necessary oil. Soon after construction a fierce gale washed away much of the sand around the base of the tower, weakening it considerably.

Ponce de Leon Inlet Lighthouse

The Seminole Indian War in the mid-1830s prevented engineers from making the necessary repairs, and the tower finally fell into the sea a year after its completion. The keeper's dwelling fared no better, primarily because the wooden building was built flat on the sand and could not withstand the wind and rising tides. One early inhabitant of the area, James Ormond III, claimed that the Indian chief Coacoochee, who was also known as Wildcat, actually had one of the reflectors from that lighthouse in his headdress during the Battle of Dunn Lawton on the banks of the Halifax River in 1836.

The great number of ships that wrecked along the coast to the north and south of the inlet reaffirmed the necessity of building a lighthouse there. It still wasn't until 1883 that the U.S. government bought ten acres of what had been the Antonio Ponce grant and assigned Orville Babcock, engineer of the Fifth and Sixth Lighthouse Districts, to build a lighthouse. When Babcock drowned the following year, General Jarrell Smith took over the construction.

In 1887, engineers finished and lighted the 168-foot lighthouse between Daytona Beach and New Smyrna Beach, after four years of hard work and numerous delays. The tower rests on a brick foundation that is 45 feet wide and 12 feet deep; the base is 32 feet in diameter and tapers upward. At sunrise the keeper drew the shades around the lens in order to prevent its discoloration and to prevent the starting of forest fires by the concentration of light of the powerful lens into the nearby trees.

Once a year a ship would bring in all of the supplies that the keeper needed, including 500 one-gallon cans of kerosene. The tower did its part in guiding mariners along the coast and decreasing the number of wrecks. During the 1920s Prohibition period, the light even enabled rumrunners from the Bahamas to sail into various safe havens, while federal revenue agents waited along the beach to try to catch them.

In 1970, the federal government discontinued use of the Ponce de Leon Light and built a more modern light at the New Smyrna Beach Coast Guard Station south of the inlet. The town of Ponce Inlet received the deed for the lighthouse and reservation property in 1972, with the hope that officials there would eventually establish a museum around the lighthouse. That same year the lighthouse, one of the tallest on the east coast, made the National Register of Historic Places. In 1982, Coast Guard officials relighted the lighthouse and placed it once again on the Coast

Guard's Light List, primarily because high rises in New Smyrna Beach were about to obscure the beacon there. On 1 November 1987, the tower celebrated its centennial.

How to get to the lighthouse

From I-95 take U.S. 92 east to South Atlantic Avenue (U.S. A1A). Turn right on South Atlantic Avenue and follow it to S. Peninsula Drive, where the lighthouse tower can be seen. Visitors can visit the museum there, walk through the keeper's quarters, and climb the 203 steps for a close-up look at the tower's lens and a breathtaking view of the surrounding area, including the Atlantic Ocean and the Halifax River. At nighttime, brilliant floodlights give the tower a majestic appearance. The museum there has lenses, equipment, local history articles, marine art, ship models, and other nautical items. Open daily 10 A.M.–8 P.M. from Memorial Day to Labor Day; open 10–5 from Labor Day to Memorial Day. Phone: 904-761-1821. Admission fee.

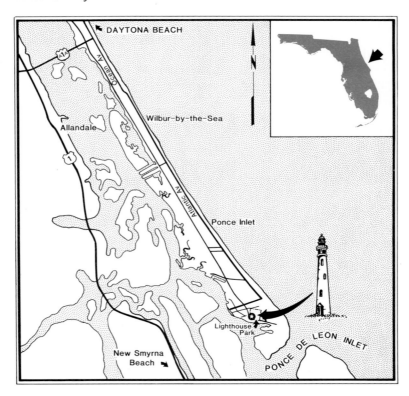

7

Cape Canaveral Lighthouse

The hook of sand that juts out into the Atlantic about 50 miles below Daytona Beach and midway down the east coast of the peninsula was the part of Florida that Spanish adventurer Ponce de Leon first sighted on 27 March 1513 as he sailed from Puerto Rico looking for gold and glory and maybe even the fabled fountain of youth. He named the area *Cabo de las Corrientes,* Cape of the Currents, after the strong offshore currents. Other explorers used the Spanish name *Canaberal* or *Canaveral,* which meant "place of reeds" or "place of cane," possibly referring to the reed arrows that the Ais Indians used to drive off Spanish explorers.

Over the next several hundred years, more wrecks in the vicinity underscored the necessity of a permanent navigational aid. Finally, in 1848, local builders who did not know much about navigational lights finished erecting a 60-foot tower at the cape, but many seamen continued to send up a chorus of complaints. They pointed out that the need for ships to sail close to shore in order to see the light actually put them in danger of wrecking on the very shoals that the light was supposed to help them avoid.

In 1853, Captain Mills Burnham became the lighthouse keeper, a position he held until his death 33 years later. Born in Vermont in 1817, he worked at various jobs in the north before heading to Florida for his health. He and his family lived a very isolated existence near the Cape Canaveral Lighthouse, having very few visitors other than an occasional shipwrecked sailor. One nonshipwreck visitor in 1857 was an eccentric Englishman, Sir Tatton Sykes, who spent time in the area wantonly killing scores of birds and trying to catch an alligator. Sykes Creek, just east of Indianola on Merritt Island, commemorates that rich, strange visitor.

Just before the Civil War, engineers began building a 145-foot iron tower to replace the first one, but war halted their work. During the Civil War, Confederate Secretary of the Navy Stephen Mallory ordered all lighthouses on the southern coast shut down to

Cape Canaveral Lighthouse

thwart attempts by federal authorities to land troops in the area and to help blockade-runners landing at night. Captain Burnham dutifully complied with the order, burying the lamps and clockwork in his orange grove near the Banana River. During the war, Burnham and his family lived off the land, raising vegetables, catching fish, and hunting game.

When the war ended in 1865, he dug up the equipment and returned it to representatives of the U.S. government, who praised him for his careful treatment of the apparatus. Workers resumed building the tower, finally completing it in 1868, installing a first-order lens that mariners could see 18 miles at sea and replacing the old whale oil fuel with kerosene. In 1873, authorities on the Lighthouse Board had the conical tower painted with black and white horizontal bands similar to North Carolina's Bodie Island Lighthouse.

When Burnham died in 1886 of measles, his family buried him in his beloved orange grove. His descendants also dedicated three stained glass windows to the memory of the Burnham family in St. Gabriel's Church in Titusville. Captain Burnham typified the self-reliant, trustworthy people who manned many of America's lighthouses.

His five daughters married some of the assistant keepers who served at the lighthouse and who went on to become keepers of lighthouses along the coast. His eldest daughter, Frances, helped her father tend the light until, in 1856, she married Henry Wilson, who became Captain Burnham's assistant keeper. Captain Burnham was succeeded by another son-in-law, George Quarterman, who in turn was succeeded by another of Burnham's sons-in-law, James M. Knight.

The sea made steady inroads toward the lighthouse, eventually getting so close that workers had to build jetties in an unsuccessful attempt to keep back the Atlantic. They eventually took the tower down and rebuilt it at its present site a mile farther inland, finally lighting the new lens in July 1894.

The Coast Guard took over the lighthouse in 1939, as it did throughout the United States. In World War II in the deep waters offshore German submarines torpedoed Allied shipping passing along the Florida coast, and that put the keepers in a dilemma as to whether to keep the light burning at night. During one period the subs sank 24 ships; Coast Guardsmen managed to rescue 504 seamen from the ships, but others were lost. Spotters in the Cape Canaveral Lighthouse, keeping a watch for the ominous explosion and flames of sub "kills," would notify the Coast Guard when they spotted a sinking ship. Authorities finally diminished the intensity of the light there and at all other lighthouses along the coast.

The lighthouse resumed full strength after the war and has continued sending out its beams since that time. Besides yachts and freighters passing along the coast, Polaris submarines also use the nearby Port Canaveral, and all take reckoning from the tall black-and-white banded tower. In 1963, President Lyndon Johnson renamed the area Cape Kennedy in honor of the assassinated president, but later authorities restored the name Canaveral, reserving "Kennedy" for the space center. Perched near the space-age gantries that send rockets to the moon and beyond, the Cape Canaveral Lighthouse harks back to a different, far less technological age.

How to get to the lighthouse

Because the lighthouse is on a military base, to visit it contact the Director of Public Affairs, Eastern Space and Missile Center, Patrick Air Force Base, FL 32925.

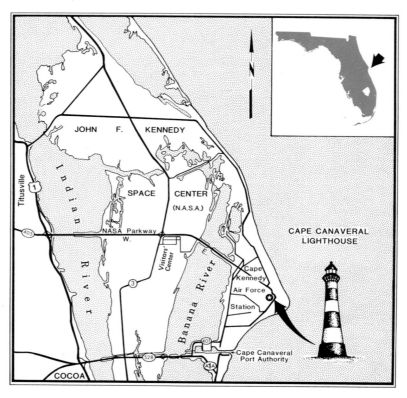

8

Jupiter Inlet Lighthouse

Seven years after Florida became a state in 1845, the Lighthouse Board attempted to make the lower coast safer for ships by recommending that a lighthouse be built near Jupiter Inlet to help mariners avoid the dangerous shoal offshore where the Loxahatchee River flows into the Atlantic Ocean. It was just north of the inlet that Jonathan Dickinson and his family were shipwrecked in 1696 on their way from Jamaica to Philadelphia. Indians discovered the twenty-four survivors and harassed them on their way north to St. Augustine, a difficult trip described in Dickinson's work, *God's Protecting Providence,* the first English account of Indians on the southeast coast. The Jonathan Dickinson State Park commemorates that man and his companions.

The lighthouse site chosen in 1853 was part of the Fort Jupiter reservation established during the Seminole War. George G. Meade, then a lieutenant in the Bureau of Topographical Engineers and later the Union general who defeated General Robert E. Lee at the Battle of Gettysburg, designed the tower. At the fort that had protected residents from problems coming from the land, the lighthouse would protect people from dangers at sea.

Among the difficulties in building the lighthouse was the silting shut of the inlet in 1854; that forced workers to send 500 tons of construction materials down the Indian River in shallow boats. The Third Seminole War interrupted work at the site from 1856 to 1858 and led workers to build the keepers' house with thick coquina walls and an inside well so that the keepers could withstand a siege. Heat, moisture, and insects further hampered the work. In 1860, after an expense of more than $60,000 for supplies and labor, the lamp was lit just before the Civil War.

During the war blockade-runners used Jupiter Inlet to ferry in supplies to the Confederacy, and Union ships attempted to stop them. Southern sympathizers wanted to prevent Union forces from using the lighthouse to find the blockade runners. They asked the

Jupiter Inlet Lighthouse

keeper to darken the light, but he felt obligated to keep it shining. A group of men that included one of the assistant keepers then disabled the light and removed the machinery from the tower in 1861 and hid it. The same men then marched to Cape Florida Lighthouse on Key Biscayne and took that tower out of service.

Federal authorities had James Armour, a volunteer coastal pilot on the federal patrol boat *Sagamore* and a man who knew the area waterways well, find the Jupiter Light's apparatus and take it by boat to Key West for safekeeping. After the war he returned to Jupiter Inlet and became the assistant keeper for two years and then head keeper, a position he kept for 40 years. When he married in 1867 and brought his bride to the lighthouse, she was the only white woman for 100 miles around. Their daughter Katherine was the first white child born in the area and went on to become the wife of the next keeper at the lighthouse. The lonely life there was interrupted once a year by a boat that delivered a year's supply of oil, paint, and other goods and by the occasional shipwreck that also provided goods, for example a sewing machine and several dogs that washed ashore after a storm.

Food supplies presented a problem to the keepers there, as at other lighthouses. Each year authorities supplied the keepers with enough flour to last a year, but weevils and worms often infested the flour to make it almost inedible. The men used to fish and hunt deer to supplement their food supplies. Indians also sold them food, charging ten cents a pound for venison. Charles W. Pierce wrote about life at that time in his *Pioneer Life in Southeast Florida* (University of Miami Press, 1970).

The government established a life-saving station near the lighthouse in 1886 to rescue people at sea. At the beginning of the twentieth century what also needed rescuing were the many migrating birds that would be blinded by the light at night and strike the tower; workers placed a screen around the light to ward off the birds. The conical tower was left a natural brick color for the first 50 years, but dampness discolored the brick so much that workers painted it red around 1910.

In 1928 an important change occurred: engineers substituted electricity for the old mineral oil lamps and cumbersome weights and installed a diesel generator in case of a power failure. In the same year a hurricane struck the tower, smashed one of the bull's-eyes, and disabled the emergency diesel generator. The keeper, Captain Charles Seabrook, had to reinstall the old mineral lamps and turn the light by hand, but an infected hand made the work very difficult. His sixteen-year-old son then volunteered to climb the tower in the storm and turn the light manually. The tower swayed an amazing 17 inches from the vertical during the storm, but the boy performed his tasks admirably. Captain Seabrook later collected the pieces of the damaged bull's-eye and sent it to Charleston to be reassembled and held together with a band of brass.

The 105-foot tower stands 146 feet above sea level, has a light that can be seen 25 miles at sea, and has walls that taper from 31 inches thick at the base to 18 inches near the top.

Jupiter Island to the north of Jupiter Inlet is an exclusive area with expensive homes inhabited by people who want to preserve much of the undeveloped land there. They have spent much money buying the north and south ends of the island and turning them over to the Audubon Society and the Nature Conservancy for use as natural sanctuaries. In that way the residents there have used their resources to protect from developers a pristine part of the coastline.

How to get to the lighthouse

From I-95 take the Jupiter exit east on S.R. 706 for approximately four miles; turn left at the end, go to U.S. 1 over the drawbridge, from which the lighthouse can be seen to the right. Take the first right after the bridge and enter the Lighthouse Park. The lighthouse and museum are open on Sundays from noon to 2:30 P.M. A marker set up by the Daughters of the American Colonists lists the names of all the early lighthouse keepers.

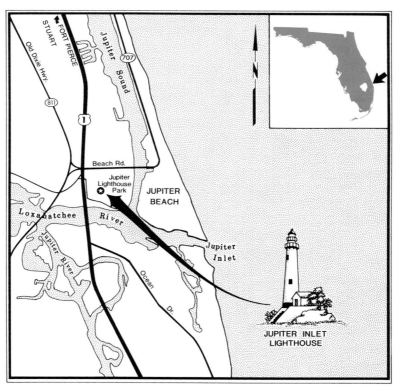

Hillsboro Inlet Lighthouse

Pompano Beach in Broward County marks the northern limit of the Florida Reef, an underwater coral formation that has wrecked many a ship on the lower east coast. The inlet there commemorates Wills Hills, the Earl of Hillsborough (1718–93), who was the British secretary of state for the colonies in 1768 when the British controlled Florida and owner of a large tract of land in Florida. His name was contracted to Hillsboro, possibly—according to local legend—to save paint.

The inlet there has proven tricky for swimmers and boaters over the years. On 11 October 1887, James Hamilton, one of the famous barefoot mailmen who carried the mail along the beach from Jupiter Inlet to Miami, came to the inlet but found that the skiff that he used to cross the water was missing. He left his mail sack and clothes on the beach, plunged into the water to swim across the 200-foot-wide inlet, and was never seen again. A shark or the strong current or even an alligator may have caused his death.

Settlers began moving into the area at the end of the nineteenth century, especially after the Intracoastal Waterway was finished to Biscayne Bay in 1890 and the Great Freeze of 1894–95 destroyed many North Florida crops. Henry Flagler extended his Florida East Coast Railroad to Miami, and in 1906 workers began draining the swamps around Fort Lauderdale. As more and more people moved into the area and more and more ships used the offshore waters, local authorities saw the need for navigational aids. Every year from 1885 until 1901 the Lighthouse Board submitted the same recommendation: "The establishment of a light at or near Hillsboro Point, Florida, would be of great assistance to all vessels navigating these waters. Steamers bound southward, after making Jupiter Inlet light, hug the reef very closely to avoid the current. The dangerous reef making out from Hillsboro Inlet compels them to give it a wide berth, and to go out into the Gulf Stream. Vessels coming across from the Bahama

Hillsboro Inlet Lighthouse

Banks would be able to verify their position if a light were placed here, a difficult matter in case they fail to make Jupiter Inlet. The establishment of this light would complete the system of lights on the Florida Reefs. The Board therefore renews the recommendation that $90,000 be appropriated for this purpose."

One of the purposes of building a lighthouse at Hillsboro Inlet was to complete the line of towers on Florida's east coast so that mariners could pass from one to the next without ever being out of range of those navigational aids. A Midwest steel firm built this particular lighthouse for the 1904 Great St. Louis Exposition, and the federal government bought the tower and second-order Fresnel lens and moved them to Hillsboro Inlet. The lighthouse was set up and the light was lighted in 1907, becoming one of the few lighthouses built in the twentieth century. The spidery structure has a cylindrical stairway in the center that protected the keepers from the weather. Engineers put such a structure at Hillsboro Inlet because the open framework would allow wind and waves to pass through without harming the tower.

The octagonal pyramidal structure has a tower that is white on the bottom third to show up against the background trees and black on the top to show up against the daylight sky. Knowledgeable local people refer to the tower as "Big Diamond" after its lantern, which consists of curved diamond panes of glass made in France.

Among the lighthouse keepers was Captain Thomas Knight, who took up duties at Hillsboro in 1911 from Cape Canaveral, where he had been born. His father, Captain Knight, and his grandfather, Captain Burnham, had both been lighthouse keepers at Cape Canaveral. Like so many sons of lighthouse keepers, Thomas Knight grew up in the service and naturally gravitated toward it.

Keepers, who had to carry the kerosene up the 175 steps, kept the light lit from one hour before sunset to one hour after sunrise. The men kept the tower clean and painted, which involved painting the exterior each year and the interior every third year. The keeper and his assistants were also to assist any shipwrecked sailors in the vicinity, going out in one or more of their three 12- to 20-horsepower gas boats and helping the survivors.

In 1932, workers changed the oil lamps to electricity and increased the candlepower to 550,000, making it one of the most powerful lights on the east coast at that time. After World War II engineers added a radio beacon. In 1966, workers installed a 1,000-watt quartz-iodine bulb, which upgraded the light to 2,000,000 candlepower. Today the iron tower rising 137 feet has an intense light of 370,000 candlepower which can be seen 28 miles out to sea on a clear night. The tower beams out a white flash every 20 seconds.

The nearby mainland section above Pompano Beach is named Lighthouse Point, commemorating the area's most prominent landmark. In 1965, dredges cut a 200-foot-wide, 800-foot-long channel through the rock reef from the mouth of the inlet out into the ocean; that provided a depth of ten feet at low tide. Spectators and fishermen along the shore can see a steady stream of boats using the inlet, especially on weekends.

How to get to the lighthouse

From I-95 take the Hillsboro Boulevard exit and go east about 7 miles. Turn right on U.S. A1A and go about 3 miles to Hillsboro Inlet. There is parking on the south side of the drawbridge and across the inlet a Coast Guard–manned station on federal property can be seen. Access is through the private property of the Hillsboro Beach Club, which has a guarded gate.

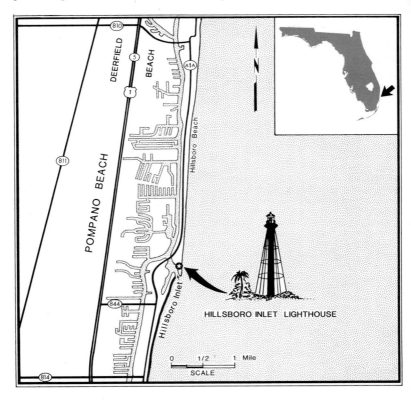

HILLSBORO INLET LIGHTHOUSE

10

Cape Florida Lighthouse

The stately tower on the southeastern tip of Key Biscayne stands quietly, yet it witnessed the most dramatic human drama seen by any of Florida's lighthouses. Commissioned by Congress after the United States acquired Florida from Spain in 1821 and built in 1825, the structure marks the reef four miles offshore and guides ships through the Florida Channel to the lee side of Key Biscayne. The builder was supposed to have constructed a 65-foot tower with solid walls of brick five feet thick at the base, tapering to two feet at the top, but he scrimped on his materials.

For the next ten years the few non-Indian settlers in the area lived an isolated life. The outbreak of the Second Seminole War in 1835 brought Indian attacks on white soldiers and settlers in Florida and the murder of the family of Cape Florida temporary light-keeper William Cooley (or Colee). Survivors fled for safety to the lighthouse and on to Key West, where the assigned keeper of the Cape Florida Lighthouse, James Dubose, was staying while the Indian threat remained. The distraught Cooley left the lighthouse to the care of his assistant keeper, time John Thompson, and a helper named Henry.

On 23 July 1836, Indians besieged the lighthouse. Thompson and Henry fled to the tower, getting in just as the Indians rushed toward them, guns blazing. Thompson stationed himself by the second window, from which he fired his three muskets at the attacking Indians and kept them at bay until nightfall. At that point the Indians set fire to the door, which soon ignited a 225-gallon oil tank. Thompson and Henry took a keg of gunpowder, bullets, and a musket to the top of the tower and began cutting away the ladder to prevent the Indians from climbing it. The raging fire forced the two men onto the two-foot-wide outside platform.

Henry died from bullet wounds, and the wounded Thompson, thinking that suicide was the best way out, threw the keg of gunpowder down the shaft. It exploded and shook the tower but did not kill him. Thompson considered killing himself by jumping

41

Cape Florida Lighthouse

off the tower but then noticed a shift in wind and an abatement of the fire. He lay still, despite the three bullet wounds in each foot, for fear that the Indians would hear him. The Indians, thinking he was dead, left the lighthouse, plundered his residence, and set it afire before paddling away. As Thompson later recalled: "I was almost as bad off as before; a burning fever on me, my feet shot to pieces, no clothes to cover me, nothing to eat or drink, a hot sun overhead, a dead man by my side, no friend near or any to expect, and placed between 70 and 80 feet from the earth with no chance of getting down. My situation was truly horrible."

The explosion of gunpowder was so loud that U.S. sailors 12 miles away heard it. They sailed to the lighthouse and found the half-dead Thompson that afternoon. It took another day before the men on the ground could figure a way to get him down from the platform, finally doing it by firing a ramrod from a musket with a length of twine attached to the ramrod. Thompson secured the twine and hauled up a two-inch rope. Two men were able to hoist themselves to the top and then lowered Thompson to the ground. They then took him to Key West, where he was treated and eventually sent to Charleston, South Carolina, to recuperate.

Cape Florida Lighthouse

When an inspector went to Cape Florida to see the damage caused by the Indians, he found that the lighthouse builders had built hollow walls for the tower instead of the solid ones contracted for, but authorities did not bring charges against anyone. The Indian threat to the area delayed a rebuilding of the lighthouse until 1846. Even then, the tower was not high enough to beam the light beyond the reefs, which the deeper-draft clipper ships that had to keep a greater distance from the Florida Reefs needed. Surveyors warned that ships would run ashore looking for the light.

In 1855, engineers raised the tower from 65 to 95 feet, but even that did not prevent ships from wrecking on the reefs. Confederate sympathizers destroyed the light in 1861. Workers repaired it in 1866, but nine years later the Lighthouse Board decided to replace it with an iron-pile structure on Fowey Rocks seven miles southeast of Key Biscayne. When the Fowey Rocks Lighthouse went into operation in 1878, the Cape Florida Lighthouse closed down.

In 1966, the state bought the 406-acre tract at the tip of Key Biscayne and established the Bill Baggs Cape Florida State Recreation Area in memory of a Miami newspaper editor who had promoted the area for a state park. Two years later the Army Corps of Engineers placed huge stones, some weighing close to a ton, in the ocean fronting the lighthouse to protect it from storm waves. On 4 July 1978, 100 years after the light was darkened, the Coast Guard reinstalled a light to serve as a navigational aid and to reduce demands for rescue services from boaters running aground while searching for the entrance to the Cape Florida channel at night. It would cost just several dollars a year to operate the small bulbs in the tower; the Fresnel lens concentrated the light so that it is seen seven miles away.

The tower is now on the National Register of Historic Places. The little ladder up the side of the tower used to extend to the ground and served as an emergency exit for the keepers. When the tower was abandoned, the ladder became a safety hazard so workers removed most of it, keeping a small portion to indicate its original appearance. The house, which replaced the one that the Indians burned in 1836, was rebuilt in the 1970s. It has two fireplaces and a sloped roof to keep the snow off, a clear indication that the house was modeled after New England houses.

How to get to the lighthouse

From U.S. 1 in Miami take the Rickenbacker Causeway to Key Biscayne, continuing south to the end of the road. There are signs to the lighthouse. Rangers give guided tours of the lighthouse compound, including the restored keeper's house at 10:30 A.M., 1:00, 2:30, and 3:30 P.M., except Tuesdays. For more information call the recreation area at 305-361-5811.

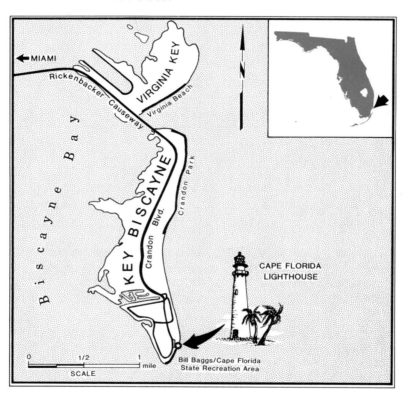

11

Fowey Rocks Lighthouse

The Florida Keys seem to be an idyllic group of islands offering unlimited fishing, swimming, and boating. They stretch from Biscayne Bay to the Dry Tortugas between Florida Bay and the Straits of Florida. The island chain, connected by some spectacular bridges, takes one from the busyness of Miami to the quaintness of Key West. The two-lane highway that connects the Keys, which gets bottlenecked in the high season or during emergency evacuations, passes by sites known in the past for killer hurricanes, Indian slaughters, and an infamous occupation—wrecking—that caused much anger and bitterness among ship owners and sailors. From time to time, travelers along that highway can see on the Atlantic side the spindly legs of the lighthouses that ring the reef along the Keys.

For over 100 years those lighthouses have been warning mariners heading north in the nearby Gulf Stream or south in the countercurrent closer to shore about the dangerous coral reef lying just off the islands. The lighthouses, about 30 nautical miles apart, permit navigators to know where they are at all times as they make their way along the Florida Keys. The site selection and construction of those lighthouses involved many hazards, but the end result made the Florida coast much safer and reduced the number of shipwrecks.

Florida was the first part of the United States discovered by Europeans but was the last settled and therefore the last on the eastern coast to have a series of lighthouses built. The disadvantage of being settled last was that for many years ships traveling up and down the poorly charted and sparsely lit Florida coast ran aground on sandbars or wrecked on coral reefs. The advantage to the late settlement was that, when Congress decided to build navigational aids along the coast, engineers could take advantage of the latest technology in both tower construction and lighting apparatus.

Designers of lighthouses for the Keys could not build the

Fowey Rocks Lighthouse

massive New England–type structure used at Anastasia Island or Ponce de Leon Inlet because of the great weight involved and because of the exposed location on the Florida Reef. The impermanence of islands off the Keys and the constant sea and wind buffeting that towers there would experience necessitated something new. Engineers came up with a skeleton framework using wrought-iron piles that had been developed in England in 1836. It offered little mass for wind and water to batter, and the foundation did not settle into sand or dirt.

Fowey Rocks got its name from the British warship HMS *Fowey*, which was wrecked on the reef in 1748. In building the

Fowey Rocks Lighthouse

Fowey Rocks Lighthouse, workers lived on a platform over the water at the site in order to minimize the danger of transporting them and their supplies out each day from the mainland. It is always dangerous to go from a boat, rocking or careening in the waves, onto a stationary platform; a misstep could cause a person to lose balance and plunge into the sea or into the iron piles. Living on that exposed platform also provided other dangers. On two separate nights the men expected to meet their deaths there when they saw steamers bearing down on them, unaware of the location of the reef. Both times the ships ran aground, further pointing out the necessity for a lighthouse there. In 1878, workers finished the 110-foot tower, which then made the old Cape Florida Lighthouse to the northwest obsolete since the new structure was in a better position to warn ships passing off the reef.

One of the assistant keepers on the new tower was Jefferson Browne (1857–1937), a young man who weathered the September 1878 hurricane at the new lighthouse. During his free time on the site in between storms he began reading law books so avidly that he apparently never took a day's vacation. After fifteen months he left the lighthouse service and entered the University of Iowa Law School, from which he earned a law degree in less than two years, a shorter time than normal because of his intense preparation while at the lighthouse. In 1880 he became the attorney for Key West and Monroe County, and in 1916 voters elected him to the Florida Supreme Court. He also wrote *Key West: The Old and the New* (1912), one of the important histories of the city.

Among the hurricanes that the Fowey Rocks Lighthouse withstood was the infamous one of 1935, which destroyed Henry Flagler's Overseas Railroad to Key West. It was so strong that it washed away the first deck of the lighthouse, 15 feet above sea level, but the tower remained standing.

More recently the Coast Guard has experimented with ways to use the natural elements around the Fowey Rocks Lighthouse to generate power that would run the unmanned light. In 1975, workers set up a windmill generator that would use the wind to turn a four-bladed propeller to generate electricity. Engineers later changed the system into a solar-powered one, making that lighthouse and others along the reefs into a low-maintenance, highly reliable navigational aid. If vandals leave the structure alone and it continues to weather hurricanes, that lighthouse should cost very little to operate.

Today the area around Fowey Rocks is part of Biscayne

National Monument, which Congress established in 1968, and it should remain protected for generations to come. Fowey Rocks, which replaced the Cape Florida Lighthouse in 1878 as a better-situated navigational aid for ships using the Gulf Stream, should help in preserving the area by warning ships to stay clear of the dangers of the area.

How to get to the lighthouse

The lighthouse is not open to the public, but those interested in visiting its vicinity can charter a boat out of Miami or Key Largo.

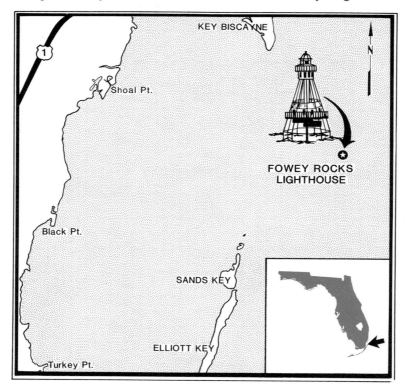

12

Carysfort Reef Lighthouse

Six miles off Key Largo stands the oldest functioning lighthouse of its kind in the United States and the first Florida Reef light to be built. Carysfort Reef got its name because of a shipwreck. The HMS *Carysford,* a 20-gun frigate, ran aground there on 23 October 1770. Carysfort Reef, like the reefs in the northern Keys, does not have sand and silt of the southern Keys that prevent a build-up of the coral. Moosehorn and staghorn coral grow in large numbers at Carysfort and coalesce into a huge wave-resistant reef that is beautiful to look at but deadly for ships that hit it. Even the coral pieces that break off accumulate in the coral colonies and solidify into a massive formation.

Because the reef was so dangerous to ships, wreckers who had long made a career of stripping the ships that ran aground on the reef made one of their headquarters in the nearby Key Tavernier. The predecessors of the wreckers were the Calusa Indians, who lived in the Keys before the time of Columbus and who preyed on wrecked ships from the sixteenth century up until 1763, when the few remaining members of the tribe were taken to Cuba as slaves.

When the United States took control of Florida from Spain in 1821 and began building lighthouses to protect shipping along the Florida Reef, that angered the wreckers, who depended on shipwrecks for a living; they resented the lighthouse keepers so much that the keepers had to avoid the wreckers as much as possible, especially when the keepers went ashore to get provisions and visit their families.

In 1824, Congress appropriated enough money to place a lightship off Carysfort Reef on the ocean side in order to provide some feasible, quick way to warn ships of the reef there. Before the days of the screw-pile lighthouse, engineers thought it would be too expensive to erect a lighthouse on the submerged reef in the Keys, so they opted for a lightship. When workers finished

49

Carysfort Reef Lighthouse

the vessel in New York in June 1825, seamen sailed it down to the Keys. Near Key Biscayne, a storm blew the ship onto a reef, the crew abandoned ship, and the notorious wreckers took possession of it and sailed it to Key West, subjecting it to the wrecking laws. For $10,000 the wreckers later sold it back to the ship's owners, who eventually anchored it off the reef.

Captain John Whalton (or Walton) of St. Augustine became keeper of the vessel for a salary of $700 a year and moved his wife and son to a small home on the northern part of Key Largo, where they had a garden and a grove of limes. Severe storms blew the ship off station, and at one point it went aground on the very reef it was supposed to warn others about. That first lightship also set a record in having the shortest time of service; after only five years it became a victim of dry rot. Authorities had to replace it with a second lightship.

When Indians attacked and burned the Cape Florida Lighthouse at Key Biscayne in 1836, forcing the lighthouse keeper to abandon the tower, the importance of the Carysfort Reef lightship increased since it was the only navigational light between St. Augustine and Key West. The lightship served the area from 1825 until 1852, but engineers were beginning to show that advanced technology was making the construction of permanent lighthouses on the reefs possible.

In June 1837, a group of Indians that had been watching the lightship attacked Whalton and three members of his staff as they went ashore to get provisions. The Indians killed Whalton and one of his men and wounded the other two, who managed to scamper into their dinghy and head out for the lightship. The Indians followed them into the water, but drenched their guns and had to give up the chase. The two crew members who reached the safety of the lightship recruited some nearby wreckers to return with them to the scene of the massacre, where they found the mutilated bodies of Captain Whalton and his companion. The crew buried the bodies on Matecumbe Key and had the Whalton family taken to Key West by mail boat. A Captain Wellington took over the lightship until the lighthouse was completed.

In 1848, the Indian troubles eased, and workers began the four-year job of constructing a 100-foot lighthouse on Carysfort Reef. When Florida seceded from the Union and joined the Confederacy in 1861, the state's lighthouse keepers had a difficult time deciding what to do about the lighthouses in their care. Their sympathies often lay with the South, but they felt an obligation to mariners to maintain the lights. The keepers at Carysfort and Sand Key decided to keep the lanterns burning, but they were probably relieved when the war ended and Florida rejoined the Union in 1868.

Beginning in 1939, Coast Guardsmen manned the lights, spending two months on duty and one month on shore leave. The Carysfort tower had the reputation of having a friendly ghost, that of a Captain Johnson who had died at the lighthouse and who supposedly returned at night to see that all was well. A more plausible explanation for the "groans" heard at night is that in the hot sun the iron walls of the tower expand; in the cool of the night they contract and make the strange noises that startle first-time visitors.

Keepers maintained the lighthouse until 1960. In order to increase the lighthouses' reliability and cut down on the cost of maintaining them, engineers looked into various experiments at automation. In the 1970s the Coast Guard installed solar panels on the Carysfort Lighthouse which transformed the sun's energy into electricty, which powered the batteries which ran the lamp. In the 1980s engineers chose a xenon flashtube beacon powered by a low voltage direct-current power supply using the sun's energy; xenon is a gaseous element used in certain electric lamps. Today the third-order light shows a group of three flashes every 60 seconds.

How to get to the lighthouse

A boat can be rented in Key Largo for the short trip to the light-house, but no one is allowed to climb onto the structure.

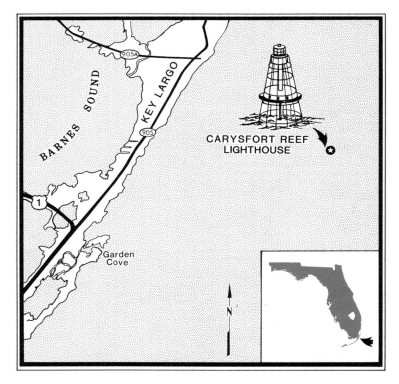

13

Alligator Reef Lighthouse

Four miles east of Indian Key is the site of Alligator Reef Lighthouse, a nine-legged white tower capped by a black lantern 136 feet above the sea. Alligator Reef is different from the reef to the north off Key Largo. The coral reef in the northern Keys is more developed than that of the southern Keys because Key Largo in the north acts as a barrier between the reef and Florida Bay, preventing sediments from the bay from reaching the coral reef.

The area has had some tragic events, from shipwrecks on the reef to pirate attacks along the Gulf Stream to the Indian slaughter on Indian Key. Nearby are the Matecumbe keys, Upper and Lower, possibly named from the Spanish *matar hombre* "to kill a man."

Pirates had preyed on passing ships in the early 1800s when Spain controlled Florida. In 1821, the U.S. government sent several experienced navy men to put an end to the pirating. When the schooner *Alligator* engaged the pirates in November 1822, its commanding officer, Lieutenant William Allen, was killed. Later the *Alligator* ran aground on the reef off Indian Key, and her crew blew her up to prevent pirates from getting her. The reef was named for that ship.

Soon after, President James Monroe asked for a special force to defeat the pirates once and for all. Commodore David Porter, who had fought Barbary pirates, commanded the new force, but it took several more years before the pirates were defeated.

Just as bad as the pirates were some of the Indians living in the Keys who resented the intrusions of whites. Indian Key became the site of a bloody Indian attack on whites. While small and seemingly inconspicuous, that island was the seat of Dade County in 1836 and had as its main resident Jacob Housman, who conducted a lucrative wrecking business up to Biscayne Bay. In 1838, Dr. Henry Perrine, a noted botanist, arrived on Indian Key with his family to conduct experiments with tropical plants. Two years later, on 7 August 1840, a large band of Indians attacked

Alligator Reef Lighthouse

the settlers, killed Dr. Perrine and twelve others, and drove off the survivors. Government troops eventually captured and imprisoned the Indians involved, but the island never recaptured its important role.

Plans for building a lighthouse in the area were postponed when Florida joined the Confederacy in 1861. It wasn't until eight years after the end of the war that workers completed the lighthouse. They used a powerful steam engine that lifted a 2,000-pound pile driver 18 feet; each blow of the hammer drove the pile one inch into the coral rock, making a sure foundation that has lasted more than a hundred years. The tower, which stands in five feet of water about two hundred yards from the deep water of the Gulf, was completed in 1873 at a cost of $185,000—$85,000 more than was first appropriated, because of the difficult working conditions and bad weather.

The logbook for that lighthouse had many notations of "squally and rainy," testifying to the awful weather conditions at that isolated post. One problem caused by the inclement weather was the inability of the keepers to return to the lighthouse by boat once they had gone ashore for provisions. An occasional notation would indicate that one of the keepers had to remain at the tower alone all night when the others could not get on board the structure.

The keeper on watch also noted many times how wreckers hovered around ships experiencing trouble. On 12 July 1874, for example, the keeper noted that a ship bound for New York with a load of sugar ran aground on Little Conch Reef at low tide. As the tide rose, the current drove the ship further onto the reef. Several wrecking schooners were in the vicinity, waiting for the ship to become completely disabled. One is reminded of the prayer of wreckers: "Oh, Lord, protect all sailors upon the sea; but if they must founder, Lord, let it happen here."

Keepers there have seen some horrific storms. The worst one, the 1935 Labor Day hurricane, had winds of 200 miles an hour, a 20-foot storm wave, and a force that killed more than 400 people in the Keys. The barometer fell to 26.35 inches, the lowest mark ever recorded in the Western Hemisphere. The day before the hurricane hit the Keys, a Coast Guard plane flew to Alligator Reef Lighthouse, near which a group of Miamians were fishing. The plane swooped low and dropped a message to the men, telling them about the approaching storm and about the need to evacuate the Keys. The men did just that and survived; many of those who refused to leave the Keys died. The lighthouse survived, partly because its spindly nature offered little resistance to the winds and waves, which passed through the supports.

The light, which is visible on a clear night 15 nautical miles at sea, was automated in 1963. A numerical system of flashes distinguishes the reef lights at night. Fowey Rocks Lighthouse at the top of the Florida Reef flashes once every ten seconds, Carysfort Lighthouse to the south of Fowey Rocks uses three flashes, Alligator Lighthouse uses four flashes, and Sombrero Lighthouse to the south uses five flashes.

How to get to the lighthouse

A boat can be rented in Lower Matecumbe Key to get to the lighthouse, but no one is allowed to climb onto the structure.

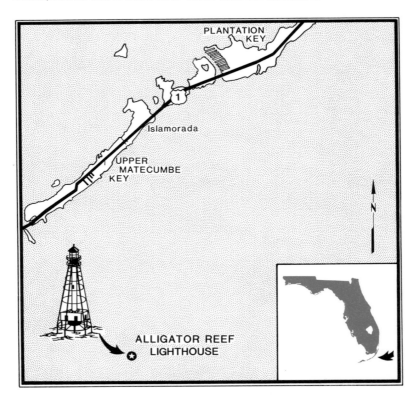

14

Sombrero Key Lighthouse

On the outer reefs near Marathon stands the tallest of the lights along the reefs, Sombrero Key Lighthouse. Situated near Molasses Key and Money Key, it is also near one of the most spectacular structures in Florida: Seven-Mile Bridge. The tower, the last reef light to be built by Lieutenant George Meade, stands 142 feet above sea level, sending out a light that ships 15 miles away can see as it flashes five times every 60 seconds.

Because the lights at Carysfort and Sand Key rotated, workers placed a first-order fixed light at Sombrero and lighted it in 1858. The structure has two platforms. The lower one, 15 feet above sea level, held two 6,000-gallon water tanks, gasoline tanks, the electric generating system, hoisting apparatus for the launch and lifeboat, and a workshop. The second platform, 40 feet above the sea, contains housing quarters, bathroom, office, kitchen, and recreational facilities that included two radios and a TV set. A cast-iron cylinder leads from the living quarters to the lantern room. Window shades protected the Fresnel lenses during the day.

Keepers usually settled their families in Key West, where they had to go to get their quarterly paychecks. Taking a boat from the lighthouse to shore involved the danger of capsizing, which took the lives of some of the keepers and also stranded those keepers left behind on the towers.

Immigrants often hired on as lighthouse keepers. The 1870 census of the Upper Keys listed the lightkeeper, Alexander Smith, from Scotland, and his assistant, John Rickleth, from Denmark. Another keeper was a German immigrant, Rudolph Reike, who served there 20 years, preferring the isolation and driving away assistant keepers who could not get along with him. His logbook entries are quite detailed, for example in noting his weekly washing of clothes and towels and oil rags. Based on the great amount of scraping, washing, and paint scrubbing the keeper noted in the logbook, it is no wonder that there was a high turnover at that

Sombrero Key Lighthouse

lighthouse. Keepers there would have agreed that lighthouse keeping was certainly not light housekeeping.

Coast Guard records from 1868 to 1899 list the improvements made to the light:

1868   Workers fitted new clamps on braces and cleared off a large accumulation of rubbish from the platform in order to give more space for fuel storage.

1869   Workers thoroughly scraped, cleaned, repaired, and painted the structure.

1874   A new hoisting apparatus was installed.

1875	Workers removed the old iron water tanks and scraped and painted the entire structure.
1881	A new wooden platform was built on the foundation, and the old ladder leading to the water was replaced by a new one.
1884	New mineral-oil lamps were put in.
1892	The keeper received a new 18-foot sailboat.
1893	The characteristic of the light was changed from fixed white to fixed white with three red sectors.
1897	Workers once again thoroughly scaled, scraped, and painted the structure.
1898	The ironwork was scraped and painted from dome to water's edge.

The logbook also noted the deaths of keepers. For example, on 18 October 1893, first assistant keeper Michael Eichhoff died and was buried at sea three days later.

In 1939, the Coast Guard replaced the three civilian keepers on Sombrero with four Guardsmen, who continued to polish the apparatus, scrape and paint the ironwork, and man the light. The men managed to keep busy during their days there by reading, sleeping, listening to the radio, working on the launch, talking with charter boat captains on the ship-to-shore radio, and checking the light. They also kept fishermen and the Marathon weatherman aware of weather and sea conditions. A telephone cable to Seven Mile Bridge kept them in touch with the Keys. Despite the rich fishing grounds around the lighthouse, the men seldom if ever fished, and never swam, mostly because of the barracudas in the area.

The men also kept their eyes open for anything unusual at sea, such as sighting Russian submarines in the Gulf Stream, intercepting alien immigrants trying to sneak into the Keys, and supplying low-on-fuel boats with enough gas to reach land. Strangely, the lighthouse also had its share of termites and ants, which might have hitched a ride on provisions, and mosquitoes, which caught a strong wind off the Keys for the five-mile trip.

One man was on duty at all times during the night. He could do his job—checking the light every fifteen minutes—not by climbing the 133 steps to the dome, but by looking up from below and listening to the steady click of a meter in the living quarters. The men worked 24 days, then had six days off, on a rotation system. In 1960, workers finally automated Sombrero Lighthouse, freeing the Guardsmen to work elsewhere and significantly lowering the cost of operating the beacon. Today its first-order Fresnel lens can be seen at the Key West Lighthouse Museum.

How to get to the lighthouse

A boat can be rented in Marathon, but no one is allowed to climb onto the structure.

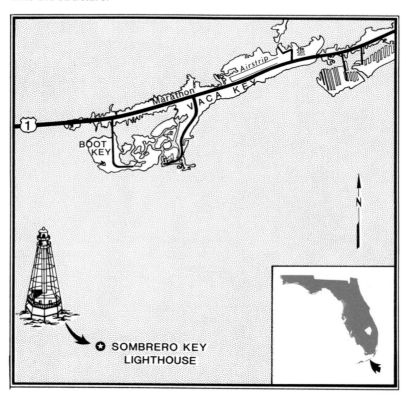

O SOMBRERO KEY
LIGHTHOUSE

15

American Shoal Lighthouse

Looking east from the Overseas Highway at Saddlebunch Keys, one can make out American Shoal Lighthouse, a structure very similar to the Fowey Rocks Lighthouse near Miami. The word "shoal" refers to a sandbank or bar which makes the water shallow. One of the characters in Hemingway's novel *To Have and Have Not* pointed out that boaters heading for the Florida Keys from Cuba will normally hit American Shoals or Sand Key to the west.

The Lighthouse Board had begun asking for a lighthouse there in the early 1870s because the strong, variable currents at that point of the reef made navigation particularly difficult for ships traveling between the Sombrero and Sand Key lights. As always it took a great deal of time to get action from Congress. In 1876, the Lighthouse Board urged Congress to take advantage of the low rates of transportation, materials, and construction, but it was not until 1878 that Congress appropriated $75,000 for a lighthouse, a figure later upped by another $50,000.

Foundry workers in Philadelphia built the parts for the light-house, completely assembled it to make sure that each part fit securely, disassembled it, and shipped it to Key West, where a special boat was built to take the parts out to the Key. It was finally ready for lighting on 16 July 1880.

The light is 109 feet above the water and is visible 13 miles away on a clear night.

It may be hard for visitors driving effortlessly over the bridges that connect the Keys to imagine how isolated the lighthouse keepers were up until the first quarter of this century. The Keys were not connected until Flagler built his railroad to Key West in 1912, so keepers were somewhat limited in how far they could go. They made regular trips to shore to get supplies, salaries, and the latest news, but the keepers themselves were quite isolated from other keepers.

American Shoal Lighthouse

The life of a lighthouse keeper might seem glamorous to some. They would work mostly at night and could spend most of the day quietly reading and fishing. They received food and lodging and had a room with an ocean view, but in actuality it was a bleak and lonely existence. They could be isolated for several months with only one companion. They might have no refrigeration or fresh food. They spent much time polishing the lenses and trying to prevent rust from weakening the structure. In the nineteenth century Indians and wreckers threatened their very lives, hurricanes were a constant danger, and they often had only one boat to depend on and to use to help ships in distress.

Cooking provided other problems in the early days. The lack of refrigeration made food spoilage a constant problem. The men had to keep eggs and butter in ice cream salt and turn them from time to time. The main staples were fish, beans, and dried foods. A favorite Sunday meal was pickled salt beef, beans, and duff (a flour pudding boiled in a cloth bag or steamed)—a delicacy imported from the British navy. Fresh drinking water was also a problem, even with a cistern or barrel placed outside to collect rainwater. Sometimes after the men had painted the lighthouse roof, paint would drip into the water barrel, causing some men to die of lead poisoning.

Yearly salaries from 1852 to 1900 ranged from $820 for the keeper to $520 for the first assistant and $490 for the second assistant. The men used that money to support their families and set up households, usually in Key West. Keepers usually spent two months serving at the lighthouse and then had a month's shore leave. The man returning from leave would bring a three-month supply of goods.

The American Shoal Lighthouse became automated in 1963 and relieved the Coast Guard of manning the structure. The Coast Guard contracted with workers to go out to the lighthouse to repair and maintain it from time to time. Some of the hired workers had been underwater treasure divers who had sought gold and jewels from sunken Spanish wrecks along the Florida reefs. During the 1980 Cuban refugee exodus men used that lighthouse to monitor the flow of boats, aid in the capture of contraband entering the United States, and evaluate a traffic-monitoring system in the Florida Straits.

Vandals who break into the towers and ransack the rooms, destroying the solar panels and batteries, cause the biggest problem currently. Such people probably do not realize how much mariners depend on the reef lights as their ships sail past in the Gulf Stream or the Florida Straits. More about this lighthouse and others along the Keys can be found in *Reef Lights* by Love Dean (Historic Key West Preservation Board, 1982).

How to get to the lighthouse

A boat can be hired in Sugarloaf Key for the trip to the lighthouse, but no one is allowed to climb onto the structure.

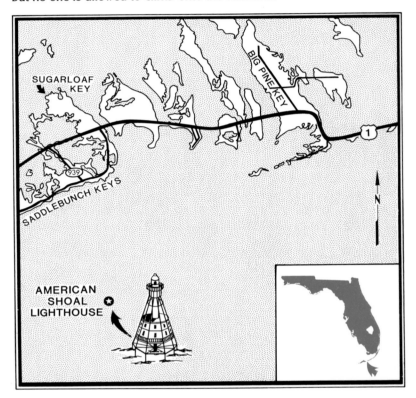

16

Sand Key Lighthouse

Eight miles south of Key West harbor lies a small sandy island that has disappeared and reappeared over the years because of high tides and strong winds. Sand Key lies near Southwest Channel, one of the main channels from the Gulf Stream into Key West. Ships using the port of Key West or continuing on in the Gulf Stream or the Florida Straits depend on the Sand Key Lighthouse, as mariners have been doing for over 150 years.

In 1827, six years after the United States acquired Florida from Spain, the federal government built a lighthouse at Sand Key but made the mistake of erecting an ordinary brick tower on the sandy island. It lasted just nineteen years, until a hurricane destroyed it in 1846.

Major John Flaherty took up his duties as lighthouse keeper at Sand Key in 1827. When he died three years later, his wife took over the post and faithfully discharged her duties and raised her family there for the next sixteen years. The 1846 hurricane that ravaged the area undermined the brick lighthouse, toppled it into the sea, and killed Rebecca and her family.

Because navigators depended on a light at Sand Key, federal authorities purchased a lightship for temporary duty there that lasted seven years while they set about constructing a new, stronger lighthouse. In 1853, workers replaced the traditional lighthouse there with a screw-pile structure, the second one in the Keys, and Latham Brightman became the keeper with two assistants. The seventeen screw piles give the structure a solid footing, and the cross members that connect the piles driven into the reef give the structure even more strength and solidity. The iron piles driven ten feet or so into the reef resemble a sword stuck into the sand up to its hilt. Large, square, iron footplates rest on top of the reef.

Because the new structure does not rest on the sandy island, it remains even after the island disappears, as sometimes hap-

65

Sand Key Lighthouse

pens. For example, a fierce hurricane that hit the island in 1865, twelve years after the lighthouse was built, washed away the sand beneath the tower, but the screw-pile structure remained standing since it was anchored into the hard rock beneath the sand. The island has reappeared and will probably disappear again in another storm, but the lighthouse should remain standing.

The keepers lived in a one-story, 38-foot-square quarters built within the framework 20 feet above the sea. Its nearness to Key West made Sand Key a favorite picnic spot in the nineteenth century. That afforded the keepers there much company and a place to settle their families. The population was very small throughout the nineteenth century. In 1830, for example, three years after the Sand Key Lighthouse was built, the census showed only 517 people in Monroe County, most of them living in Key West.

In 1902, keeper Charles Johnson also acted as a warden to note the numbers and types of nesting birds in the area and warned people not to kill the birds or steal their eggs. It was typical of the way keepers became involved in protecting the environment, whether marine or animal.

Coast Guardsmen check the light, which was automated in 1941, every three to five months. The present light, which replaced the fourth-order Fresnel lens in 1982, projects out from its perch 109 feet above sea level 13 miles on a clear night. The huge tankers that steam along in the Gulf Stream still use the friendly light to guide their way away from the treacherous reef lying just under the surface.

The particular light characteristics of Sand Key Lighthouse are two light flashes every 15 seconds. In the last 20 years the lighthouse has probably served as a beacon for those fleeing Cuba in boats, dinghies, and makeshift rafts. A museum in Key West has actual boats used by the refugees who fled under cover of darkness from Cuba, 90 miles away. Harry Morgan used the light as a bearing as he came from Cuba to Key West in Ernest Hemingway's novel *To Have and Have Not.*

The damage that the 1846 hurricane did to Sand Key reminds one how vulnerable the Keys are to Atlantic storms. The Labor Day Hurricane of 1935, Hurricane Donna in 1960, and Hurricane Betsy in 1965 hit the Keys with some of the strongest, most intense winds and waves ever experienced along the Florida coast. Though the U.S. Weather Bureau developed more sophisticated, accurate warning devices between 1935 and 1960, a hurricane nevertheless remains unpredictable. A quick change of course can take it to unprepared sites, and the narrow highway linking the Keys can become congested with late evacuees. That the lighthouse at Sand Key and other like it can withstand winds up to 250 miles per hour testifies to the technical advances and skills of nineteenth-century lighthouse builders.

Kirk Monroe, a nineteenth-century Florida writer, wrote the following poem about the lights along the Keys:

> The fixed *white* light of Fowey Rocks,
>   And Carysfort's *white flash,*
> Both may be seen from the middle
>   Of a twenty-three mile dash.

Alligator Reef's *red, white* and *white*
    Lies thirty miles away.
Log thirty more, Sombrero *white*
    Points to Honda Bay.
Then comes the Shoals American,
    White flashing through the night,
Just fifteen miles from *white* Key West,
    Twenty from Sand Key's *twinkling white* .
The Marquesas are unlighted;
    But on Rebecca's Shoal,
A *white* and *red* is sighted,
    Warning from wreck and dole.
Sixteen miles to Dry Tortugas
    With a *white* light on the fort,
Three more to the *flash* of Loggerhead,
    And all's clear to a western port.

How to get to the lighthouse

A boat can be hired in Key West to go to Sand Key, but no one is allowed to climb onto the structure or camp on the island.

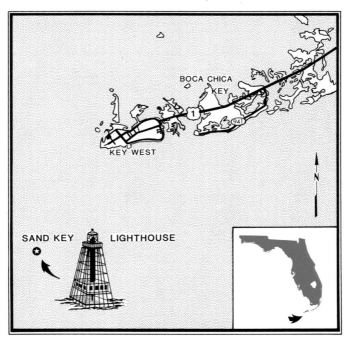

17

Key West Lighthouse

The southern tip of U.S. 1 ends in a town that once had the country's highest per capita income and thriving cigar and sponge industries and was the largest Gulf of Mexico port. The town still draws a million visitors a year and celebrates a make-believe secession from the U.S., but inflated real-estate prices have driven many old-timers away.

The name Key West comes from Spanish *cayo hueso* (bone island) because of the many human bones found there by Spanish explorers in the sixteenth and seventeenth centuries, bones of shipwrecked sailors and/or victims of Indian raids. Lieutenant Commander Matthew Perry took possession of Key West in 1822 with instructions to examine the island and report to Washington on the dangers to navigation. In his report he stressed the need for lighthouses on the Florida Keys, suggesting as sites Cape Florida, Key Largo, Sand Key, and the Tortugas.

Wreckers made a living working out of Key West, especially after the U.S. Congress set up a federal court there in 1828 to decide the salvage claims of the wreckers. Their ranks were made up of New England sailors, Bahamian immigrants, and local fishermen. Many of them were honest salvagers, but many were unscrupulous, greedy scavengers who lured ships onto the reefs. Other industries flourished in the town, including cigar making and sponge fishing, but labor troubles, hurricanes, and a decrease in navy personnel greatly affected the town's fortunes. Several severe outbreaks of yellow fever killed off many of its settlers and made the place unfit for habitation.

By an act approved 7 May 1822, Key West joined St. Augustine and Pensacola as three Florida towns to have customs districts. The customs collectors, as superintendents of lighthouses in their districts, were in charge of constructing and repairing lighthouses, procuring and placing beacons and buoys, recommending persons for appointments as keepers, and disbursing funds.

Key West Lighthouse

As extra compensation for their duties in that regard, they received 2.5 percent commission on the lighthouse disbursements.

The first lighthouse in Key West was a 65-foot tower built in 1825 on Whitehead Point, and the first lighthouse keeper was Michael Mabrity, a pilot. When he died in 1832, his wife, Barbara Mabrity, took his place, partly because she knew the job well and also because she needed to support her six fatherless children. Mrs. Mabrity served as keeper at Key West from 1832 to at least 1861. In the early days of the lighthouse service it was highly un- usual for women to serve as lighthouse keepers. As male keepers died, leaving widows with no other immediate means of earning a living, more and more women applied to become keepers, since they had come to know the job well while they helped their husbands. In 1861, fifteen women served as lighthouse keepers in the United States, but the number decreased after the Civil War as heavier fog-signal equipment began to be used in the towers.

The 1846 hurricane destroyed the lighthouse and killed fourteen people who had sought refuge in the tower; Barbara Mabrity survived, but seven members of her family died. The next year builders put up a new 66-foot tower, the present lighthouse, on higher ground and more inland to protect it from storms. Later William DeMeritt became the keeper and kept the job for 43 years. Still later William Bethel became the keeper, and, when he died, his wife, Mary, took over his duties.

As the city grew around the lighthouse, tall buildings and trees threatened to obscure the light, so, in 1894, workers added 20 feet to the tower, making it 86 feet tall. Because the base of the tower is about 15 feet above sea level, the light is 100 feet above sea level.

When Henry Flagler's Overseas Railroad reached Key West in 1912, the town became much more accessible to the mainland. Ferryboats carried train passengers from Key West to Cuba, but despite Flagler's expectations the railroad did not make Key West a major port to points south and west. Trains served the town regularly until the disastrous 1935 hurricane wiped out much of the railroad. The federal government then bought up the bridges and built an Overseas Highway for cars in 1938.

When the Coast Guard removed the lighthouse from active service in 1969, the Key West Art and Historical Society took it over as a museum. On exhibit there are the first-order Fresnel lens from Sombrero Key Lighthouse, ship models, old photographs, military uniforms, and nautical charts, all of which give a good picture of the island's maritime traditions. More than 150,000 visitors visit the lighthouse each year, a number that has taken its toll on the tower. In 1989, workers restored the lighthouse to its turn-of-the-century appearance, preparing it for the beginning of the celebration of the bicentennial of the Lighthouse Service, established 7 August 1789.

A lighthouse-like structure to the northwest of Key West was the Pilot House, a house on stilts that marked the northwest channel. Built in 1855 to accommodate harbor pilots waiting to board incoming ships and guide them to safe harbor in Key West, the house was rebuilt in 1879 and remained in use until 1932. At that time the light and buoys set up by the Coast Guard to mark the channel made the Pilot House unnecessary, and it was abandoned. Ernest Hemingway and other fishermen found shelter there during storms. It burned down in 1971, probably the action of vandals.

How to get to the lighthouse

Take U.S. 1 into Key West, continue on North Roosevelt Blvd. to Truman Avenue to Whitehead Street. The lighthouse/museum is at 938 Whitehead Street. Visitors to the top of the tower get a panoramic view of the town and ocean. Museum open daily 9:30 A.M.–5 P.M. 305-294-0012. Admission fee.

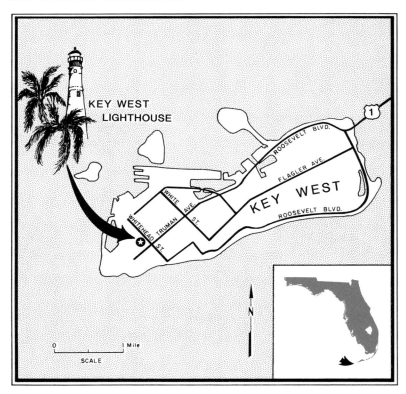

18

Garden Key Lighthouse

Visitors arriving at Fort Jefferson by air from Key West are in for a breathtaking sight. As they approach Garden Key, 70 miles from Key West and 120 miles from any mainland, seemingly in the middle of nowhere, they will see a huge fort, a half-mile around with each of the fort's six sides 450 feet long and 50 feet high. The surrounding 70-foot moat that used to be 30 feet deep supposedly had sharks to dissuade would-be escapees.

In 1513, when Ponce de Leon first discovered the rocky islets that lie 70 miles west of Key West, he called them Las Tortugas (The Turtles) because of the many turtles found there, turtles which replenished the dwindling food supply of the Spanish explorers. Later sailors called the islands the Dry Tortugas because of the heat and dry conditions.

Pirates used the islands to hide in and dart out from to prey on the many ships using the channels off the islands; pirates may also have buried treasure on the islands, a persistent rumor seldom if ever substantiated. In 1821, the U.S. Navy ousted the pirates and began to consider the feasibility of building a lighthouse on one of the islands. Four years later engineers built the first lighthouse on Garden Key.

The first Garden Key lighthouse keeper, William Flaherty, brought his wife there, but she hated the boredom, heat, and mosquitoes so much that she complained to the wife of President John Quincy Adams. Soon after, William Flaherty was assigned to a mainland lighthouse.

Federal authorities realized that a powerful force occupying the Dry Tortugas could control Gulf navigation to the Mississippi Valley, so one year after Florida became a state (1845), the U.S. Corps of Engineers began building Fort Jefferson on Garden Key. Work continued for 30 years and used more than 40 million bricks, but the fort was never finished. Its eight-foot-thick walls surround what was to be the largest in a chain of seacoast

Garden Key Lighthouse

fortifications from Maine to Texas that the U.S. government built in the first half of the 1800s. Up to 1,500 men could garrison there, although the average number was 500.

James Fenimore Cooper's novel *Jack Tier, or the Florida Reef* (1848) is set at the Garden Key Lighthouse. During the action of the novel the keeper and his assistant were kidnapped and killed by foreigners, with the result that the lighthouse remained darkened for nights on end, a potentially tragic event for many navigators depending on the light for guidance.

Workers later transported the lighthouse onto the battlements of the fort where it served as a harbor light for Tortugas Harbor. The most famous ship of the squadron stationed there, the U.S. battleship *Maine,* was sunk in Havana harbor in 1898, an action that precipitated the Spanish-American War. The first boat that reached the scene to take off survivors may have been *The Mangrove,* a lighthouse tender captained by P. O. Cosgrove of Key West.

During the Civil War, the federal government housed military prisoners in Fort Jefferson, including Dr. Samuel Mudd, the Maryland physician who had innocently set the broken leg of John Wilkes Booth, Abraham Lincoln's assassin. Sentenced to life imprisonment, Mudd was pardoned in 1869 after he helped fight the 1867 yellow fever epidemic that ravaged the fort.

When authorities built the nearby Dry Tortugas in 1858, they moved the first-order lens from the Garden Key Lighthouse. The Dry Tortugas Lighthouse was one of the few southern lights that stayed in operation during the Civil War, primarily because federal troops occupied the key during that time.

The army abandoned Fort Jefferson in 1874 after another fierce hurricane and another fever outbreak. In the late 1890s it stationed a few troops during the Spanish-American War, and the navy built a coaling station there, but storms continued to weaken the structures. In 1908, the area became a wildlife refuge for sooty terns, birds that come by the thousands to lay eggs on the nearby islands. In 1912, fire destroyed the lighthouse keeper's house. In 1935, President Franklin Roosevelt named seven islands in the area a national monument, rescuing the fort from the decay that abandonment brings.

Ernest Hemingway's short story "After the Storm" (1932) takes place to the east of Garden Key. It is about a ship that sank during a storm as it tried to go between Tortugas and Rebecca Shoal at night. The captain miscalulated, and the ship hit the quicksands in the area and sank, with a loss of over 450 people. Hemingway's mention of Rebecca light refers to the old Rebecca Shoal Lighthouse that stood on the southwest edge of the shoal. It consisted of a small white house and square skeleton tower with the light 66 feet above water.

Workers first began constructing the Rebecca Shoal tower there in 1855 but were greatly hampered by rough seas and strong winds. It was completely destroyed in 1858 and had to be rebuilt. After the houselike structure was completed in 1886, it remained totally exposed to the elements, which gradually took their toll. Today a modern beacon stands there marking the dangerous shoal.

The knobby little lighthouse tower seems insignificant on the walls of the vast fort, but it has served its purpose well as a harbor light to the many boats that use the harbor. Even today, one can find a dozen or so sailboats and yachts anchored nearby on any day, taking advantage of the peaceful area for swimming, snorkeling, and bird-watching.

How to get to the lighthouse

The fort, open during the daytime, has a museum, a slide show, and a self-guided tour. For information on flights from Key West, see the Key West Chamber of Commerce.

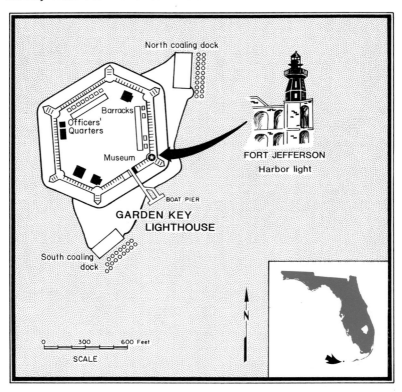

19

Dry Tortugas Lighthouse

Three miles west of Fort Jefferson is Loggerhead Key, named for the loggerhead turtles that used to nest in abundance there where the Atlantic Ocean and the Gulf of Mexico meet. The picturesque little island, the largest in the Tortugas, has Australian pines, coconut palms, and cactus. It used to have a bar that soldiers from Fort Jefferson would frequent on payday, but the bar is long gone. The 151-foot brick tower, built in 1858, has walls that are six feet thick at the base and taper to four feet at the top. Because the construction of the tower took place from 1856 to 1858, four years before the Emancipation Proclamation, it is probable that slaves worked on it.

When an 1873 hurricane damaged the tall tower, engineers drew up plans for a new structure, but repairs to the old one were so good that the new plans were never used. Part of the reason for the tower's longevity is the fact that, unlike nearby Fort Jefferson, which is slowly sinking into the sea, Dry Tortugas Lighthouse has a firm foundation. It consists of beams laid crosswise underwater and a three-foot-high concrete foundation that used expensive, hard bricks that could resist the harmful sea air better than cheaper bricks from the North. The 203 steps to the top led to a first-order Fresnel lens that beamed out the light from a 1000-watt bulb to ships 28 miles away. The lens has been removed from the Dry Tortugas tower and is on display at the U.S. Coast Guard Aids to Navigation School in Yorktown, Virginia. The light displays a modern optic with the same 28-mile visibility.

Ernest Hemingway's novel *To Have and Have Not* (1937) mentioned that the Dry Tortugas Lighthouse had a two-way radio, so that key would not be a good place for runaways to land. Hemingway spent much time around the Keys fishing and boating and probably came to know the lighthouses well.

During World War II, because lighthouse keepers worried about being attacked by German submariners in search of food

77

Dry Tortugas Lighthouse

and oil supplies, the Coast Guard stationed six extra men to protect the light.

When Dry Tortugas Light Station was manned by Coast Guard personnel, two guardsmen stood a ten-day duty. They were relieved at the end of their ten days by two other personnel of the Aids to Navigation Team, Key West. The frequency of their duty at the island depended on the number of personnel attached to the ANT and the repeated requests from guardsmen who enjoyed the assignment.

Before the light was automated, the Coast Guard assigned five men to the lighthouse on 18-month shifts. Because of rotating leaves and time off, usually only two or three men were on site, and they had duty 12 or 24 hours at a time. For every two days they were on duty, they got one day off the island.

The primary duties of the men, who lived in a three-bedroom house near the tower, consisted of taking care of the light, which beams out from sundown to sunup; maintaining a radio beacon for ships and aircraft; monitoring the emergency radio channels; and every three hours radioing in the weather conditions to Key West for the National Weather Service.

Maintaining the rotating beacon, three electricity-producing generators, the grounds, and quarters kept the men quite busy. They had several dogs that provided a semblance of security to the island, especially at night. A Coast Guard ship brought in fresh water and fuel each month. Leisure activities on the island, where pleasant year-round temperatures range between 65 and 85 degrees, included swimming, snorkeling, and fishing, but life could be pretty monotonous.

The Dry Tortugas Lighthouse, white on the lower half and black on the upper half, is the least accessible of Florida's lighthouses. Part of its significance lies in the fact that it is the last American lighthouse seen by ships heading into the Gulf of Mexico from Key West and the first one seen by ships heading into Key West.

Today that massive tower continues to aid ships passing offshore; with luck it will last another hundred years.

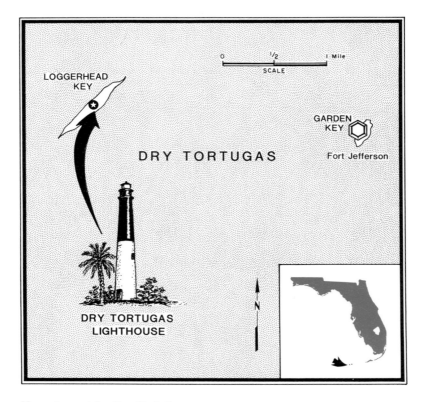

How to get to the lighthouse

After reaching Fort Jefferson by plane or boat, visitors should check with the rangers there to see about visiting that particular day. They can then boat across to the island.

20

Sanibel Island Lighthouse

Drivers crossing the Sanibel Causeway can look to the eastern end of the island and catch a glimpse of a four-sided pyramid tower that has been guiding ships in the Gulf for more than 100 years. Before the construction of the causeway in 1963, a ferryboat took visitors and automobiles across the bay. Two famous winter residents from Fort Myers, Thomas Edison and Henry Ford, liked to make the trip and spend a relaxing day on the beautiful island.

A history of the Sanibel Lighthouse shows how slowly the government bureaucracy moves. In 1833, a small group of settlers from New York asked the federal government for a lighthouse, but nothing happened. Twenty-three years later (1856) the Lighthouse Board asked for a lighthouse there, but still nothing happened. Twenty-one years after that (1877) government surveyors examined Point Ybel on the eastern tip of the island and closed the area off to private ownership. They said that the end of the island was a natural place for a lighthouse because navigators used it as a reckoning point as they entered and left the busy port of Punta Rassa.

Six years later (1883) Congress approved plans for a lighthouse and appropriated $50,000 for the work, but authorities learned that Florida, not the federal government, owned the land; Florida Governor W. D. Bloxham ceded the land to the federal government, but it took another two years to get the lighthouse finished. One final snag developed when the ship carrying the tower's ironwork from New Jersey wrecked two miles from Sanibel. A diving crew from Key West salvaged most of the pieces, and the lighthouse was completed in August 1884. It wasn't until four years later that Sanibel was opened to homesteaders, and the island got its first resort hotel, the Casa Ybel.

Part of the importance of a lighthouse on Sanibel was the fact that Punta Rassa, a nearby deepwater port on the mainland, was a cattle-shipping point from the 1830s until the Spanish-American

Sanibel Island Lighthouse

War began in 1898. Because no railroads served the area until the 1880s, ranchers drove cattle overland to the port and shipped them out to Cuba and Key West by schooner. The shipping congestion led to more demands for a lighthouse, since there was none between Key West and Egmont Key near Tampa.

In 1884, Dudley Richardson of Key West became the first lighthouse keeper; his assistant was John Johnson. In 1888 or 1889, Henry Shanahan, a former seaman and carpenter, arrived from Key West with his wife and two small sons; two years later he replaced Johnson as assistant keeper. When Richardson resigned in 1892, Shanahan applied to become the keeper, but authorities at first refused to hire him because he could not read or write. They finally relented when he made it clear he would not stay on as an assistant. He went on to serve as keeper there for 22 years. He and his first wife had seven children. When she died, Henry married a widow with five children, and then she and Henry had one more, for a total of thirteen children. When he died in 1913, his son Eugene took over the duties as keeper, and Henry's stepson, Clarence Rutland, served as assistant keeper from 1936 through 1941.

Sanibel Island Lighthouse

Lighthouse duties did not vary much from day to day; each morning the keeper or assistant would extinguish the flame, trim the wick, polish the lens with its seven prisms, wind the clockwork mechanism that kept the light revolving, and curtain the prisms to protect them from the sun and to prevent fires in the woods below from being started by a concentration of the beams from the lens. In the evening one of the men would climb the 127 steps to the watchroom and touch a flame to the wick to send the beam out to sea. A second man would relieve the first at midnight. Life eased a little in the early 1940s when workers converted the light to acetylene gas with a valve that used the sun's rays to turn the beam on and off.

When workers built the lighthouse in 1884, they also built two detached frame houses on firmly based iron columns. The houses, joined to the lighthouse by a stairway, have wide verandas extending around the buildings on three sides. The houses and the lighthouse are Sanibel's oldest surviving buildings, having withstood many storms, high tides, and gale winds. During hurricanes local residents flocked to the safety of the lighthouse, confident that the structure would protect them. One time 11 Cuban fishermen came ashore during a fierce gale and sought refuge in the compound. The two cottages became headquarters for the J. N. "Ding" Darling National Wildlife Refuge in 1950.

When the Coast Guard took over operating and maintaining lighthouses in the United States from the lighthouse service in 1939, the Coast Guard Light Attendant Station in Fort Myers took charge of the Sanibel Lighthouse. At one point the Coast Guard announced that it would discontinue operating the lighthouse unless it could be shown to be useful. As often happens in such situations, local residents became concerned about the possible loss of the island landmark, convinced the Coast Guard how important it was to them, and succeeded in keeping it operating. Today the Coast Guard lists the light as a seacoast light for offshore purposes.

In 1952, someone placed a TV antenna on top of the tower, and that enabled local residents to see their first television on the island. In 1962, workers converted the tower to electricity, but the light went out soon after when a mercury switch failed, and the tower remained darkened for a week, the first failure in 78 years. Twelve years later the lighthouse and keepers' quarters made the National Register of Historic Places. The City of Sanibel now operates the lighthouse property under an agreement with the

Coast Guard. City employees live in the cottages rent-free in return for some maintenance and supervision of the property.

How to get to the lighthouse

From Fort Myers head west for Sanibel via S.R. 867 and the Sanibel Causeway, a toll road. At the four-way stop sign on Sanibel, turn left on Periwinkle Way and drive 4.8 miles to the end of the island, where there are signs to the lighthouse. Visitors can walk around the lighthouse and keepers' quarters but cannot enter the actual grounds.

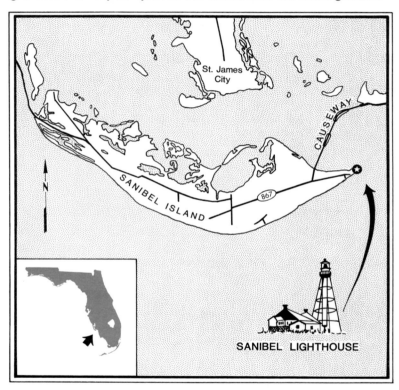

SANIBEL LIGHTHOUSE

21

Port Boca Grande Lighthouse

At the southern tip of Gasparilla Island off the coast of Charlotte County sits a houselike structure called the Port Boca Grande Lighthouse that guards the entrance to Charlotte Harbor and the busy channel and points the way to the 60-foot-deep pass and its famous tarpon fishing. Boca Grande Pass, off the southern tip of Gasparilla Island, marks the entrance to Charlotte Harbor. Gasparilla Island took its name, so the story goes, from a renegade Spanish naval officer, José Gaspar. Gasparilla Island and Little Gasparilla Pass, as well as Tampa's annual Gasparilla Festival, all take their names from him.

In 1822, Gaspar and his pirates ran down what appeared to be a large British merchant ship. Just as the pirates were about to board the ship, it lowered the English flag, ran up the U.S. flag, and began firing point-blank into the pirate ship. With the end in sight, Gaspar wrapped himself in an anchor chain and threw himself overboard to his death. Ten of the crew were later hanged, but a few on shore escaped.

It's a nice story that local writers like to embellish, but Gaspar the pirate probably never existed. He seems to have been concocted by a hermit, John Gomez, who lived around 1900 on Panther Key in the Ten Thousand Islands south of Fort Myers. It is also possible that a Spanish missionary priest in the 1500s, a Friar Gaspar, was the real source of the name Gasparilla.

The elegant town of Boca Grande on the six-mile-long Gasparilla Island means 'large entrance' or 'big mouth' in Spanish and refers to the nearby wide passage to the Gulf. It is through that wide, deep, and easily navigated pass that large freighters have been going into and out of Charlotte Harbor for years. A long pier for phosphate ships extends into the deep water to the east of the point. The sheltered port two miles from the Gulf of Mexico was dredged deep enough to accommodate large ships. Traffic at the port there increased substantially in the 1880s when phos-

Port Boca Grande Lighthouse

phate discoveries in west-central Florida and advanced mining techniques led to larger shipments of the mineral from Boca Grande to ports elsewhere. In the 1890s barges transferred phosphate from the Peace River area to oceangoing vessels in deep water off the coast. Besides the lighthouse, workers built a dock and a customs office that would inspect incoming vessels about to load the phosphate.

In 1888, Congress appropriated $35,000 to the Lighthouse Service to build a lighthouse on the southern tip of Gasparilla Island, and it was completed two years later, when workers built on a pile foundation a one-story, white frame dwelling with a shingled roof. On top was a black lantern that displayed a fixed white light interrupted by a red flash that warned ships of the hazardous Boca Grande Pass. A similar building, but without the lantern, about 70 feet away, was for the assistant keeper.

Because the light, which was first operated on 31 December 1890, was to serve as a harbor beacon rather than as a necessary light for boat traffic farther out in the Gulf, it could be relatively lower than other towers along the coast.

In the 1950s and 1960s the sea reclaimed more than 600 feet

from the middle of the island and another 1,400 feet from the southern tip. A road along the western edge of the island, which had been several hundred feet from the Gulf in 1940, was quite close to the water in 1970. Residents of Gasparilla Island formed the Boca Grande Conservation Council, which led the fight to stop the erosion and enlisted support from the many winter residents, including U.S. Senator Mike Mansfield of Montana. The Gulf waters, which had washed away more than a million square feet of shore and were threatening homes, were actually flowing around the supports of the abandoned lighthouse, threatening to topple it into the sea during the next big storm. Vandals also did much damage to the abandoned buildings, stripping the electrical wiring and breaking the windows.

Local property owners who wanted to prevent further erosion felt stymied because the federal government, which owned the southern end of the island, including the land that the lighthouse sat on, seemed reluctant to spend any money on a structure it considered outdated and useless. Shipowners feared that the continuing erosion would fill the channels in Boca Grande Pass and endanger the large freighters using the port. The Boca Grande Pilots Association supported the efforts of the Boca Grande Conservation Council to reverse the erosion of Gasparilla Island, especially because a sandbar emerging in the water off the island close to the channel was posing a threat to ships.

In 1971, the government contracted with a construction company to build a granite groin at the southern tip of the island, and workers built a 265-foot jetty into the Gulf to help restore the beach to its former depths. The local utility company, which owned the nearby fuel depot at Port Boca Grande next to the five-acre lighthouse site, pumped some 100,000 cubic yards of fill into the sea, including 35,000 cubic yards around the lighthouse. In 1972, the federal government transferred ownership of the lighthouse to Lee County, which planned to make it part of a park. The county commission had contractors correct the tilt of the lighthouse and began making plans to refurbish the building. In 1980, the lighthouse made the National Register of Historic Places, and in 1986 the Coast Guard installed the old, rebuilt light in the lantern. With concerted efforts of local residents, historic preservationists, and a public-spirited utility company, workers were able to save the lighthouse. Local officials restored the building to its former condition, making the beacon once more an aid to navigation.

Unlike the massive towers of Anastasia Island, Ponce de Leon Inlet, and St. Marks or the screw-pile structures along the Florida Keys, the squat, broad Port Boca Grande Lighthouse was adapted by engineers to its site. Since the lantern itself did not have to be very high, it sat atop the house-type building and was easily accessible to the keeper. Although not open to the public, the beautiful structure can be photographed from outside its enclosing fence.

How to get to the lighthouse

From Venice or Port Charlotte head for Placida below Cape Haze. At Placida follow signs for Boca Grande. After crossing the toll bridge and driving to a four-way stop sign, turn right and go around to the left along the road that borders the Gulf. Continue from the Range Rear Lighthouse for approximately two miles to the Gasparilla Island State Recreation Area. Just beyond the parking lot a dirt road leads to the right, where visitors can see the lighthouse and walk around it on the beach.

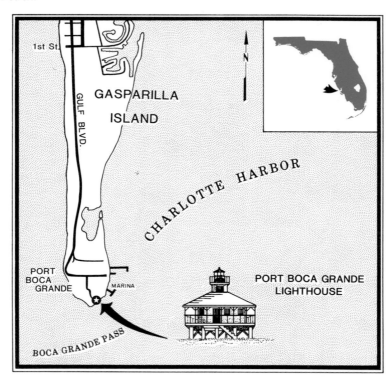

22

Boca Grande Lighthouse
(Entrance Range Rear)

About a mile north-northwest from the lighthouse at the southern tip of Gasparilla Island is a tall, gangly, pyramidal structure with a black lantern 105 feet above mean sea level. The Boca Grande Lighthouse, also called the Entrance Range Rear Lighthouse, is higher than the Port Boca Grande Lighthouse in front of it. When a ship lines up the two lights so that one is directly over the other, the ship is in midchannel. Workers completed the structure in 1890, the same year as the Port Boca Grande Lighthouse, but a shifting of the channel later put the lighthouse in the Gulf 50 feet from the beach. Workers then moved the tower to a spot 175 feet from the high-water mark on a range with the outer buoys. An 18-foot boat was also located at the lighthouse for the keepers to use.

The lighthouse served the area well, especially when Gasparilla Island was an important phosphate port and a favorite vacation resort for wealthy visitors from the north. Phosphate made the island an important port at the beginning of this century and led to the building of the two lighthouses. In 1885, geologists discovered phosphate near Bartow, Florida, west of Lake Wales and south of Lakeland, and began mining it. Phosphate companies needed a quicker, more efficient way of getting the mineral to Charlotte Harbor than simply taking it by slow barge 75 miles down the Peace River to Punta Gorda and Charlotte Harbor. A railroad direct to Boca Grande would do much to speed the mineral on its way to factories elsewhere.

By 1909 workers completed the dock and railroad at Boca Grande, including two major trestles connecting Gasparilla Island to the mainland. In 1925, Seaboard Coast Line bought the line and dock for $5.22 million and continued hauling phosphate to the dock until late 1979. Building the dock and the railroad depot

Boca Grande Lighthouse

in the center of town northeast of the range rear lighthouse did much to develop the little town of Boca Grande on the island.

A more important, longer-lasting development has been the lure of the island for tourists and winter residents. In 1913, when the elegant Gasparilla Inn was finished and awaited its first tenants, a Boston dowager tried to make reservations at the inn and was surprised when the manager asked for "social references" for her. His request amused the woman so much that she told her friends about the inn that accepted only the "right kind of people." The word spread fast, and soon the Drexels and Biddles and DuPonts began frequenting the place. Some of those families later bought land on the island and built some of the beautiful winter homes that one can glimpse along the beachfront. In 1917, traffic increased so much that workers enlarged the inn and added a casino. In the 1940s, trains like the Silver Star and the Palm Land took travelers from New York to Boca Grande in 26 hours, transporting them from the harsh northern winters to semitropical days and sandy beaches.

Tarpon fishermen continued to flock to the area to take advantage of the excellent fishing, especially in the summer months when the fish were biting and accommodations were more readily available. Wealthy residents and fishermen have returned repeatedly to the island, making it one of the most exclusive resorts on Florida's west coast but one that has escaped the hordes of tourists that gravitate to the state's east coast.

Up until 1958, one could reach the island only by boat or train, a fact that added to the isolation and exclusivity of the resort. In that year, workers built the Boca Grande Causeway, which made the island more accessible to tourists and residents, especially when the Seaboard Coast Line discontinued train service to Boca Grande.

While not as elegant as some of the more famous Florida lighthouses, the Boca Grande Lighthouse has served the area well. The spiderweb structure enables it to withstand the winds and storm tides that kick up from the Gulf. It is the last lighthouse before the one at Egmont Key near St. Petersburg, and, while visitors cannot climb its stairs to the top, the base of the tower remains one of the most accessible. One can walk up to it, around it, and below it on the beach.

The closeness of the lighthouse to houses and the road points up another problem with lighthouses today. As the tower's beacon receives more and more competition from lights—from nearby houses, shopping malls, or high-rise condominiums—navigators at sea have to depend on their modern electronic equipment that can pinpoint their location and warn of impending, unseen reefs. Engineers have realized this for some time and have been making use of the country's many strategically placed lighthouses, installing in them radio beacons in order to help ships sailing along the coast.

How to get to the lighthouse

From Placida follow the signs to Boca Grande. After crossing the toll bridge and driving to a four-way stop sign, turn right and go around to the left along the road that borders the Gulf. The lighthouse is less than a mile from the stop sign and about a mile from the Port Boca Grande Lighthouse at the tip of Gasparilla Island.

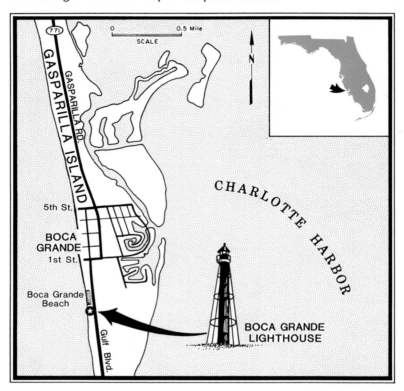

23

Egmont Key Lighthouse

The history of this little island in the middle of a very busy shipping lane goes back quite far. The great Spanish sailor, Ponce de Leon, may have seen it in 1513 as he cruised up the Florida coast. Other early visitors were probably Spanish explorers Panfilo de Narváez in 1528 and Hernando De Soto in 1539. It received its name in 1754, when the British surveyor, George Gauld, named it after John Perceval, second Earl of Egmont and First Lord of the Admiralty (1763–66) during the British occupation of Florida.

Visitors to isolated Egmont Key off Bradenton, St. Petersburg, and Tampa can scarcely imagine how important the place was in the nineteenth century. During the 1830s residents in Key West and Sanibel asked the federal government to erect a lighthouse in Tampa Bay, but it wasn't until 1848 that engineers built one. That same year Colonel Robert E. Lee made a survey of the southern coast and, recognizing the military significance of the island, recommended that defensive works be erected. In September of that year a fierce hurricane covered the island with six feet of water and damaged the new lighthouse. The keeper and his family escaped harm by lying in the bottom of a boat tied to a tree, but after the storm, when he looked at his damaged lighthouse, he rowed off to Tampa and never returned.

A second hurricane a few weeks later further damaged the tower and continued the erosion that threatened to undermine the structure and topple it. In 1858, workers tore the structure down and built a new, stronger one on the old foundation for $16,000. That white tower is still standing today on the northern end of the key and has weathered several strong hurricanes. Engineers built the tower with three-foot-thick brick walls and with nooks and crannies for storing goods or hiding from attack.

The size of the 398-acre island, only 1.6 miles long and a half mile wide, belies its importance. That size has changed over the years, depending on erosion and wave action. Lying only three

Egmont Key Lighthouse

or four feet above sea level, the island is subject to wind and waves but manages to support a thriving colony of turtles, 18-inch lizards, and rattlesnakes, as well as lots of poison ivy. The water near the island varies in depth, reaching 90 feet off the northeast corner. Egmont Channel, Tampa Bay's main shipping channel, serves several thousand ships a year as they go to and from Tampa and St. Petersburg.

Authorities used Egmont Key in the 1850s as a temporary holding area for Indians being shipped to Indian Territory west of the Mississippi. At the beginning of the Civil War Confederate blockade-runners used the island as a base until Union forces captured it in July 1861. Then Union troops used the island as a base from which they attacked ships and installations in the Tampa area. The federal government also kept Confederate Navy prisoners on the island and started a cemetery there in 1864 for Union and Confederate veterans. When the cemetery closed in 1909, authorities removed the bodies to national cemeteries elsewhere.

Out of fear of a possible Spanish invasion during the Spanish-American War in 1898 and as part of a comprehensive coastal defense system, engineers built on the island a large coastal artillery installation, named Fort Dade, in honor of Major Francis L. Dade, the army commander whose detachment was slaughtered by Seminole Indians in 1835. Fort Dade's heavy battery at the north end of the island, together with Fort DeSoto's mortar batteries on Mullet Island to the northeast, dominated the main ship channel that led into Tampa Bay. A battery of smaller weapons on the south of Egmont Key protected a secondary channel. With those batteries in place the military in essence took over the island. Authorities used the island hospital to quarantine all American soldiers returning from Cuba, having them spend ten days for observation purposes.

In World War I, Coast Artillery units of the National Guard used Fort Dade on Egmont as a training center. Besides the fort the island had a school, a post office, a jail, several miles of brick streets, and about 600 people at its busiest. By 1921, when planners considered elaborate coastal defense installations obsolete, the government deactivated Fort Dade.

During World War II, the military again began using Egmont Key, that time as a harbor entrance patrol station and as an ammunition storage facility for vessels entering Tampa Bay. The military also used the island for amphibious warfare and aerial gunnery exercises.

After World War II the military once again abandoned the island except for the Coast Guard that tended the lighthouse. In 1974, Egmont Key became a National Wildlife Preserve, which helped protect the hundreds of gopher tortoises making their home on the island. In 1978, it joined the National Register of Historic Places, primarily because of the lighthouse.

When the Coast Guard manned the lighthouse, three or four men took turns caring for the light, usually in shifts of two men for a two-week period. Each day just before sunset and just after sunrise one of the keepers flipped a breaker switch in a shed at the base of the lighthouse to turn the beacon on or off, instead of climbing the stairs to the top as in days past. The men lived in a three-bedroom, air-conditioned, concrete-block house. They had a fully equipped kitchen, a washer and dryer, TV, VCR, pool table, dart board, computer, and stereo, the last bought through something called the "keepers' morale fund." The men also maintained the Federal Aviation Administration radio beacon that guides commercial air traffic into the Tampa Bay area airports. They aided the island's owner, the U.S. Fish and Wildlife Service, by protecting the island's wildlife. The men fished, snorkeled, and swam to relieve the monotony of a post the Coast Guard labeled "semi-isolated."

How to get to the lighthouse

The lighthouse can be reached by boat. There is no public dock, but small craft can be anchored on the beaches. The lighthouse can be seen from Fort DeSoto Park three miles away.

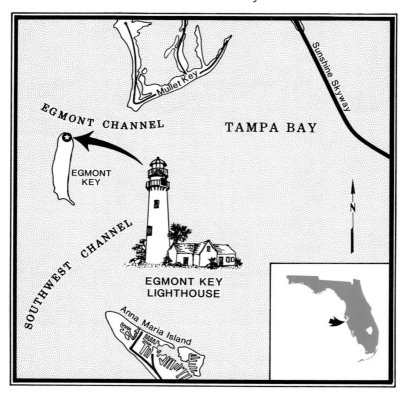

24

Anclote Key Lighthouse

Because the currents and tides along Florida's west coast are weaker than those along the east coast, Florida's Gulf of Mexico lighthouses, while reliably lighting the way for navigators, have a less dramatic flair about them than do the state's Atlantic lighthouses. However, the Gulf coast lighthouses have seen their share of hurricanes, and much more so than the northeast coast of Florida, partly because the open waters of the Gulf have generated many storms and partly because Gulf hurricanes often have a tendency to circle back or curve into the western coast. Thus Tampa and Cedar Key have seen far more hurricanes than have Jacksonville or St. Augustine.

Anclote Key off the western coast near Tarpon Springs has the distinction of being in two counties: Pasco and Pinellas. The federal government owns the island, which is now a state park and a wildlife refuge. The 180-acre island is about 2.5 miles long and has vegetation consisting of oaks, pines, and shrubs. The word *Anclote,* which comes from Spanish and means 'anchor, grapnel, kedge,' gave its name to Anclote Key and the Anclote River. Spanish boats full of fish used to sail into the harbor at Anclote to take on fresh water before the long trip to Cuba, where they sold their fish. Anclote later became a sponging center and, still later, a fishing port. Mullet and grouper ran in the summer and mackerel, trout, and bluefish in the winter.

In 1885, Congress appropriated $17,500 to build a lighthouse at Anclote Key, but because it was to be similar to Florida's Cape San Blas Lighthouse, which cost $35,000, authorities asked for an additional $17,500, which Congress appropriated in 1886. The lighthouse, which guarded the mouth of the Anclote River, was built in 1887 on the southern tip of Anclote Key. The first light was fueled by kerosene.

Anclote Key Lighthouse, which is abandoned and unlit, has been turned over to the State of Florida as part of Caladese State Park.

Anclote Key Lighthouse

Originally two families lived on the island to tend the light-house. During the Spanish-American War in the late 1890s the lightkeepers had a small cannon for self-defense, but they remained free of siege or attack. One keeper kept pigs on the island, letting them wander at will, which worked fine until some Cuban boat crews came ashore and stole the pigs. Mosquitoes were a big problem on the island, even after WPA crews dug drainage ditches to reduce the summer insect populations. The logbook indicated from time to time that the bugs kept the keepers from working outdoors.

Because the island was so close to the mainland, the keeper

or his assistant frequently went by boat to Anclote or Tarpon Springs. Several times a week one or the other man went across the short stretch of water to attend church or get provisions or pick up the mail or visit family or attend a party. The island also had more visitors than most such sites, especially on weekends as picnickers sailed over for a day at the beautiful beach.

The logbook was also unusual in that it almost never mentioned weather conditions or ships passing offshore. Instead, the keeper usually noted what work he and his assistant did around the tower, like cutting the grass, building a fence, polishing the lens, or taking off for a day of fishing.

The logbook also hid the feelings of the keeper during traumatic events. On 6 October 1889 the keeper noted: "Baby was taken very sick at 5 P.M.," referring to his child. The entry for the next day was very brief: "Baby boy died this morning at 2.30 oclock. Keeper and wife went over to bury him to-day." Likewise, the next year on 30 August, the joy of a new arrival was passed over as the keeper simply noted: "Baby born. Keeper's wife. Bad weather."

This lighthouse and the one at Seahorse Key to the north would have assumed a greater importance in directing Gulf traffic if the Cross-Florida Barge Canal had become a reality. Partly because of pirate raids and the deadly reef along the Florida Keys and because some early out-of-staters looked on Florida as an obstacle to go around or through to get ships from the Mississippi River to the eastern shore of the United States, shipowners decided to cut a ship canal across north Florida. The canal would begin at Yankeetown up the coast from Anclote and use the Withlacoochee, Oklawaha, and St. Johns rivers on its way to Jacksonville and the Atlantic.

Men and mules began digging the ship canal in 1935. If it had been finished, it would have brought salt water from the Gulf and the Atlantic into the limestone rock that supplies water to South Florida. In 1936, after much debate, work on the canal stopped, but advocates of a barge canal, whose locks and barriers would keep out saltwater intrusion, took up the fight.

When German submarines began sinking ships in the South Atlantic, the Caribbean, and the Gulf during World War II, canal supporters pestered Congress for money to build a protected waterway across the state. The Army Corps of Engineers, with authorization from Congress, resumed building the canal by constructing locks and dams, but a large group of concerned citizens, the Florida Defenders of the Environment, marshaled scientists and legislators into opposing the plan. The canal was finally killed in the 1970s, but every once in a while it rises from the dead to become an issue.

Anclote Key Lighthouse no longer operates as a functioning aid to navigation and has been abandoned by the Coast Guard. The construction on the mainland of a tall, industrial smokestack, lighted with strobe lights, eliminated the need for the lighthouse as a major aid to navigation in the area.

How to get to the lighthouse

From Tarpon Springs go north on Alt. 19 for 0.3 mile. Take a left on Anclote Road, a winding, at-times brick road for 2.5 miles to Anclote River Park, from which a boat can be taken for the three-mile ride to the south end of Anclote Key. The lighthouse, which cannot be seen from the park, is still on Anclote Key, but the keepers' quarters are gone.

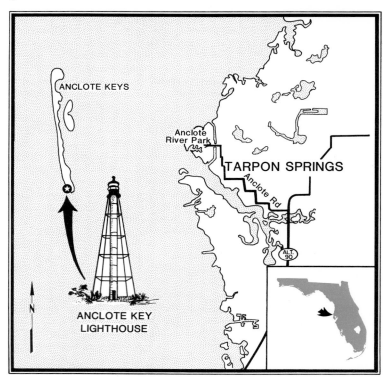

25

Seahorse Key Lighthouse

The little island of Seahorse Key, with its squat lighthouse sitting on a high hill, has the most intriguing ghost stories of any of Florida's lighthouse sites, stories involving a headless horseman and a drowned girl who turned into a white mule. Situated about three miles west-southwest of Cedar Key and between the Gulf outlets of the Suwannee and Waccasassa rivers, Seahorse Key is about a mile long and at most half a mile wide. Its name, which is far more alluring than the nearby Deadman's Key or Snake Key, comes from its shape or the shape of a high dune on the island, at 52 feet one of the highest elevations on the Gulf coast. Indians used the island at least a thousand years ago, as evidenced by their relics and shell mounds.

As do so many Florida islands Seahorse Key has legends of buried treasure. One in particular has a pirate named Pierre LeBlanc and his palomino guarding the treasure of the pirate Jean Lafitte around 1800. Lafitte had given LeBlanc the horse from a shipment of horses he was taking to New Orleans. One day a snake hunter came ashore to collect some of the many snakes on the island for sale to those who collected snakeskins. LeBlanc discovered him but after some misgivings began to spend more time with the stranger.

After several days and evenings spent together, sharing a bottle, telling stories, and becoming friends, the snake hunter managed to ply his friend with more than the usual amount of liquor while remaining sober himself. When the inebriated LeBlanc finally mounted the palomino to make his nightly rounds of the island, his friend followed him and discovered the pirate's sea chest full of jewels.

When LeBlanc passed out near the treasure, the stranger opened the chest and began scooping out the jewels into his burlap bags. LeBlanc then awoke, shouted an oath at the thief, and attacked him with his sword. The hunter staggered back, managed to wrestle the cutlass from LeBlanc, and with one

101

Seahorse Key Lighthouse

swoop severed the pirate's head from his body. The hunter grabbed up some of the jewels, fled to his boat, and made his escape, but not before looking back to see LeBlanc's horse pacing the shore. To this day some locals maintain that late-night visitors to Seahorse Key can see a headless horseman making his rounds on a tall palomino.

The other story associated with the island deals with a beautiful young lady from Cedar Key who fell in love with a ne'er-do-well sailor. He took her on his ship, killed her, and pushed her body overboard. Her body was never found, but about that time a white mule appeared on Seahorse Key. Some fishermen believe the mule is the ghost of the girl.

In any case, the lighthouse there may have had a forerunner when the followers of dissident William Augustus Bowles built a watchtower on the island about 1801. Bowles was the self-styled "Director General of the State of Muskogee," a would-be independent state located between the Apalachicola River and St. Marks in the Panhandle. Some of Bowles's pirates/followers set up an outpost in the Cedar Key area and put up a watchtower to keep a lookout for Spanish warships or prey. The watchtower lasted until a Spanish naval expedition destroyed it in 1802.

During the Second Seminole War (1835–42) federal troops used Seahorse Key as a detention camp for Indians being transferred to the West for resettlement. The federal government, realizing how strategic and useful Seahorse Key and several other islands in the vicinity were, reserved them for military use. In the 1840s, Cedar Key was becoming a major shipping port for cedar, pine, cypress, rosin, and turpentine. Ships also stopped there to get fresh supplies of good water. The depth of the harbor encouraged entrepreneurs, like pencil manufacturers who harvested the cedar trees growing on the keys, to make plans for more development, and navigators began asking the federal government for a lighthouse. In 1850, Congress appropriated $8,000 for a lighthouse on Seahorse Key, adding another $4,000 in 1852.

Lieutenant George Meade, who later led the victorious troops that defeated Confederate troops at the Battle of Gettysburg, helped design the lighthouse on Seahorse Key when he served with the Topographical Engineer Corps of the U.S. Army. Workers built the brick structure in 1854 on granite rock pilings and used solid wooden shutters to protect the windows. Later, workers added wooden-frame housing wings to each side of the brick tower for the lighthouse keepers and their families. The light was 28 feet high, which placed it some 75 feet above sea level, and had a fourth-order fixed light visible for 15 miles.

William Wilson became the first keeper in 1854. At the beginning of the Civil War Confederate sympathizers extinguished the light to hinder Union forces that were blockading the coast. In 1861, federal troops occupied the island and turned the lighthouse into a prison. A cemetery on Seahorse Key contains the graves of sailors stationed there and the wife of one of the lighthouse keepers. After the Civil War, engineers relighted the light, which resumed helping ships using the Cedar Key port.

In the last half of the nineteenth century Cedar Key had several chances at rapid development, but timing and nature worked against it. The state's first Atlantic-to-Gulf railroad from Fernandina to Cedar Key, which David Yulee completed in 1861, was destroyed by soldiers during the Civil War. Second, forestry companies didn't conserve the timber and palm fiber around Cedar Key and left when the resources were depleted. Third, Henry Plant considered building his railroad to Cedar Key and making the small town into a major port but couldn't reach a satisfactory agreement with the town and, instead, built his line to Tampa, which became a major Gulf port. Finally, a severe hurricane and tidal wave in 1896 greatly damaged Cedar Key.

In 1905, the navy installed a wireless telegraph station on Seahorse Key. Ten years later, the light there was extinguished permanently. Later, Seahorse Key became part of a National Wildlife Refuge, which helped protect the more than a thousand endangered brown pelicans that live in the area. The University of Florida now uses the island for marine biology research.

How to get to the lighthouse

Seahorse Key, which lies three miles west-southwest of Cedar Key, is a U.S. Department of Interior wildlife refuge and not open to the public.

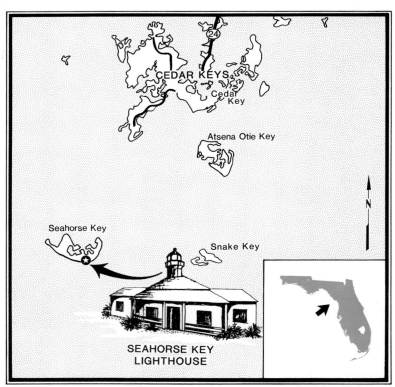

SEAHORSE KEY
LIGHTHOUSE

26

St. Marks Lighthouse

The ride to St. Marks Lighthouse along a seven-mile, winding road through pristine swamp and wilderness is probably the most beautiful to any land-based Florida lighthouse. As the white tower begins to take shape in the distance, marking the end of land and the beginning of the Gulf, one can begin to appreciate how isolated the keepers and their families lived one hundred years ago.

The tranquility of the scene masks its stormy history. First, the early Spanish settlers built a wooden fort there in 1680. If they had also built a lighthouse, and we have no record of it, it would have predated the 1716 building of the Boston Lighthouse, which is generally recognized as the first in the United States. In 1718, the Spanish established the town of St. Marks, probably on the feast day of St. Mark. In 1759, they built a masonry fort, San Marcos de Apalache, which William Augustus Bowles and his band of Indians captured in 1799. The Spanish retook the fort, and then in 1819 General Andrew Jackson captured it. The port there, which is 30 miles south of Tallahassee, grew in importance until the Civil War.

In 1827, navigators who used the Gulf of Mexico near the growing towns of Magnolia, Port Leon, Newport, and St. Marks petitioned Congress for a lighthouse at the mouth of the St. Marks River, where it flows into Apalachee Bay. Two years later workers began using the limestone brick from the nearby ruins of Fort San Marcos de Apalache to build a lighthouse. When they finished the structure in 1829, the local customs collector would not accept it because the tower walls were hollow. It took two more years to complete the structure to the satisfaction of the customs collector, who accepted it in 1831. In the winter of 1842 workers relocated the structure more inland away from the encroaching waters that were undermining the tower. The next year they added a small, four-room dwelling for the keeper. During the Seminole Indian

St. Marks Lighthouse

Wars the keeper requested a bodyguard and an escape boat, but authorities denied both requests. Fortunately, the Indians did not realize how vulnerable the keeper was or at least did not take advantage of it.

Twenty years later, during the Civil War, Confederate troops were stationed near the lighthouse to defend the area from Union troops. In 1865, 1,000 Union troops landed there on their way to the Battle of Natural Bridge near Tallahassee, where the Confederates beat them back. Tallahassee remained the only Confederate capital east of the Mississippi that did not surrender to Union forces. After the Civil War workers rebuilt the tower and house, finishing the job in 1866.

One family that served at St. Marks Lighthouse, the Greshams, had the distinction of taking care of the tower from 1892 to 1957. They had a very isolated life since the area was accessible only by boat and seaplane, but they seemed to thrive on it. The Gresham children who grew up at the lighthouse looked back on their days there as carefree, but also full of hard work and books: carefree in that they could wander over the sand dunes, swim in the surf whenever they wanted to, and catch fish with their bare hands; full of hard work and books because they had many duties around the lighthouse and because they were expected to keep up in their studies. Their own private schoolteachers lived with them during the summer in the simple four-room house. One teacher, a young man named E. W. Roberts from Mississippi, fell in love with one of the keeper's girls and married her when she turned twenty-three.

Another of the girls at age fifteen fell in love with a tall, handsome man from St. Marks who fished in the area. They began meeting in secret because she knew her father would not approve of the man. Four years later she left her family and eloped with the man. The marriage ended in divorce, as her father had predicted.

Once a week in their 14-foot dinghy propelled by a three-horse engine, the Greshams would go seven miles to St. Marks for groceries and supplies. Later they acquired a 19-foot boat with a 12-horse engine. The isolation of the lighthouse, especially during the bad winter months, forced the children to entertain themselves and not depend on outsiders for companionship. In the evening they would go along the water's edge and pick out whatever fish they wanted for dinner that night, or the boys would shoot some wild geese or ducks. Marsh hens were a particular family delicacy.

Visitors who dropped in from time to time to spend a few days with the family included Governor Cary Hardee from Tallahassee, hunters from Pensacola, and the Ringlings from Sarasota, who arrived by yacht. Mable Ringling once paid a $400 hospital bill for the keeper's family because Mr. Gresham had helped her kill a wild goose. At Christmastime the Ringlings and the Pensacola hunters sent the children lots of gifts. During Gulf storms fishermen and Greek spongers from Tarpon Springs sought shelter at the lighthouse or in nearby coves.

The sturdy lighthouse tower is 82 feet high and rests on a 12-foot-deep base made of limestone blocks taken from the ruins of Fort San Marcos de Apalache. The walls are four feet thick at the base and taper to 18 inches at the top. The scratches in the reflector light are supposedly from the time when Confederate troops took it down from the tower and hid it in the salt marsh. It was automated in 1960 and joined the rest of the unmanned beacons that the Coast Guard visits and maintains periodically.

St. Marks Lighthouse is in St. Marks National Wildlife Refuge, established in 1931. The refuge has 65,000 acres of land and protects an additional 32,000 acres of Apalachee Bay. One can see some 300 species of birds in the park, 98 of which nest there.

Protected birds include the Southern bald eagle, osprey, and red-cockaded woodpecker. Because the lighthouse is in a wildlife refuge, it will remain in an undeveloped stretch of coastline, which will give the structure a grandeur and serenity missing from more congested sites.

How to get to the lighthouse

From U.S. 98 take S.R. 59 south into the St. Marks National Wildlife Refuge. The lighthouse is at the end of the road, seven miles from the visitor center. It is usually not open to the public, but visitors can walk around it. Admission fee to the refuge. The visitor center is open Monday through Friday, 8 A.M.–4:30 P.M.; Sunday, 10 A.M.–5 P.M. The center has displays, a bookstore, and information packets. Phone: 904-925-6121.

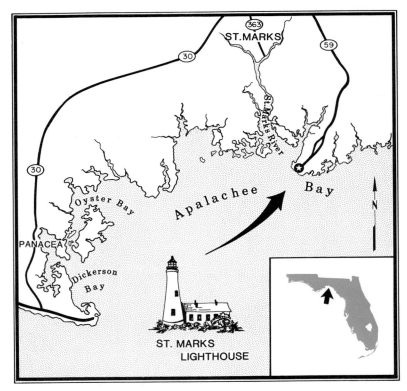

ST. MARKS
LIGHTHOUSE

27

Crooked River Lighthouse

The skeleton tower that now sits outside the town of Carrabelle in Franklin County replaced one on Dog Island off the coast. One should know the history of the latter in order to appreciate the difficulties engineers had in building and maintaining the Crooked River Lighthouse.

Guarding the entrance to St. George Sound in the Gulf of Mexico, Dog Island may have gotten its original name, Isles aux Chiens, from wild dogs on the island when the French explored the area in the 1500s or from its supposed shape of a crouching dog. The seven-mile-long, 2,000-acre island once housed a federal government facility that included a lighthouse and quarantine station for ships using the port. Today the island serves as a vacation spot for tourists and some residents.

In 1838, workers built a lighthouse on the west end of Dog Island, installing a revolving light to distinguish it from the Cape St. George Lighthouse to the southeast. The exposed nature of the site led to damages from gales in the 1840s and from fire set during the Civil War by Confederates who wished to prevent federal troops from using it as a lookout post. Soldiers also used the lens for target practice.

In 1872, continued buffeting from storms pushed the tower one foot out of perpendicular, which necessitated the removal of the lens to the top of the keepers' dwelling. The following year a hurricane toppled both the tower and the keepers' dwelling into the bay, where they remain to this day, covered with water.

Congress approved $20,000 to rebuild the tower, but the money was never spent when the Lighthouse Board decided that local commerce was not developing enough.

More than 70 years after the collapse of the lighthouse, developers subdivided Dog Island and sold lots to people who were usually unfamiliar with the geologic history of the place. Hurricane Agnes and other storms battered the island, destroying

Crooked River Lighthouse

the houses built on the sand and forcing new owners to build on stilts. Researchers have discovered that in the last hundred years the western half of the island has moved north and west, that is, toward the mainland.

Geologists boring beneath St. George Island discovered ancient oyster beds, indicating that the barrier island is about 4,100 years old and has shifted over the centuries. If there is a significant warming trend in the future, scientists predict that water will cover the barrier islands, causing much damage and possibly destroying the islands for good. In any case, the Apalachicola delta continues to inch outward toward the islands. The point to be learned from the studies of geologists and from the demise of Dog Island Lighthouse due to encroaching Gulf waters is that the barrier islands have been shifting their position over thousands of years and probably will continue to do so.

The town of Carrabelle in Franklin County on the mainland is protected to some extent by the barrier islands. The town was named in 1897 in honor of a local woman, Carrie Hall; first named Rio Carrabelle, it later dropped the Rio. Crooked River, which gave its name to the new lighthouse, empties into the Ochlockonee River to the east and the Carrabelle River to the west. Heavy lumber trade from the Apalachicola River to Crooked River prompted authorities in the 1880s to request a lighthouse to replace the Dog Island Lighthouse, destroyed in 1873.

Congress authorized the spending of $40,000 in 1889 for a lighthouse in Carrabelle, but uncertainty over the land title and a fire that destroyed many important documents postponed construction until 1894–95. Workers finished the structure in August 1895, and the fourth-order lens 115 feet above sea level began operating on 28 October.

The relative unimportance of the town and lighthouse allowed the keeper to have only one assistant, whereas other sites had two assistants. When something serious took one of the two keepers away from the Crooked River tower, the other person had to take up the slack. For example, when the assistant keeper's wife in Carrabelle became seriously ill in May 1897, he left the lighthouse to be with her. From 12 May through 25 May, each day's notation in the logbook began the same way: "Assist Keeper absent." The keeper, James Williams, had to do all the duties at the site during that time.

Despite the depth of Crooked River and despite the plans of local planners who foresaw a burgeoning port, the area never fulfilled the expectations of developers, especially as Apalachicola to the south began to grow. The interior land behind Carrabelle, part of which is known as Tates Hell Swamp, remained undeveloped, and only a small community grew up around the lighthouse. For years Carrabelle's claim to fame has been the state's smallest police department, a tiny office beneath a chinaberry tree at the corner of U.S. 98 and S.R. 67.

During World War II, in order to avoid the German submarine threat off the Florida coast, workers built a gasoline pipeline in Franklin County to transport products to Jacksonville that arrived in Carrabelle by barge. At the end of the war, that pipeline was discontinued and dismantled. In 1947, the town lost its railroad and further retrenched economically. With a 1980 population of 7,661, an increase of only 8.4 percent since 1970, Franklin County is one of the smallest counties in the state. In 1980, Carrabelle had a population of only 1,304, up only 158 people in twenty years. The port there used to handle cotton from Georgia and tropical hardwoods from Central America for processing in the United States, but today that port is relatively quiet.

Carrabelle is the eastern terminus of the north Gulf coast's Intracoastal Waterway. From there to Tarpon Springs, where the waterway takes up again, the mariner must pass over 200 miles of open Gulf, with few protected harbors and shoals extending five or six miles out from the shore.

Today motorists traveling southwest of Carrabelle can see the skeleton-tower lighthouse to the right of the highway up a dirt road. In a way it represents a town that has always looked to the sea for its livelihood, whether shipping, fishing, shrimping, or oystering. If the area revives, it will probably be once again because of the sea, but more from people seeking its beaches and offshore islands.

How to get to the lighthouse

Driving southwest from Carrabelle on U.S. 98, one can look to the right a mile outside of the town to see the tower.

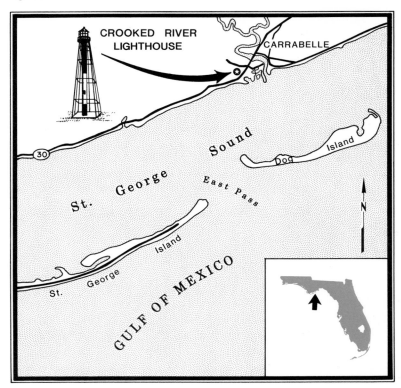

28

Cape St. George Lighthouse

Apalachicola Bay is a fairly well protected body of water about 25 miles long and six miles wide. It produces about 90 percent of the state's commercial oyster harvest and much of its fish products. The bay has five passages to the Gulf of Mexico: East Pass (just west of Dog Island and south of Carrabelle), St. George Sound, Sikes Cut, West Pass, and Indian Pass. Fresh water feeds into the bay from the Apalachicola River.

Cape St. George, St. George Island, and St. George Sound were probably named by the English for the patron saint of England and thus commemorate a saint in the Anglican Church rather than the Roman Catholic Church. St. George Island is a 3,000-year-old barrier island between two others that separate the Gulf of Mexico from Apalachicola Bay. Its many miles of beaches with sea oats and sand cliffs are particularly beautiful and un-spoiled. Situated on the southwest part of the island that juts into the Gulf of Mexico, Cape St. George Lighthouse has lighted the way for mariners passing offshore and also for those wishing to enter the western part of Apalachicola Bay. The island is actually increasing in size ever so slowly because of sand deposits at Cape St. George and East Pass.

The lighthouse guides those boats heading to and from the town of Apalachicola on the mainland. That town, one of the most important ports in territorial Florida, was the home of Dr. John Gorrie (1803–55), the physician who developed an ice machine that was the forerunner of the modern refrigerator. He used air-cooling machines to help patients suffering from malaria and yellow fever. His machine circulated air over ice to cool a room, but, because he could not get a reliable supply of ice, he made a machine to make artificial ice. He is one of two Floridians honored in the Statuary Hall of Fame in Washington, D.C. (the other being General Edmund Kirby Smith of Civil War fame).

When authorities realized how important a lighthouse would be on Cape St. George and Congress authorized the money,

Florida Lighthouses

Cape St. George Lighthouse

workers built a 65-foot tower on Little St. George Island in 1833, and it remained until a new tower two miles away replaced it in 1847. Its third-order lens was visible 15 miles at sea. Wind pushed it over in 1851, to be replaced by a new tower in 1852. Although damaged during the Civil War and during hurricanes, that white brick conical tower still stands today.

Engineers who designed the newest tower and keepers' quarters paid particular attention to the strength of the buildings—with good results. Whereas an earlier tower had only 18-inch-deep foundations, much too small for the buffeting that the tower took, the new 72-foot tower had solid pilings to rest on. The thickness of the walls varies from four feet at the base to two feet at the top. For the interior and exterior walls workers used hydraulic cement, a mixture of lime and clay which hardens under water. The tower's six windows are reinforced with strong frames and iron bars. A circular stair leads from the ground to within six feet of the lantern, with an iron ladder completing the ascent. In 1878, workers built a keepers' quarters so well that, soon after completion, it withstood a hurricane without suffering any damage.

Cape St. George Lighthouse

The keeper had an assistant, and the two of them would split up the watches each night, one taking the sundown-to-midnight watch one night, and the other taking over at midnight. The next night the two men would switch the watches. The keeper made fuller logbook notations than most, especially as he described wrecks, for example, on 16 February 1888: "Schooner came from the eastward loaded with lumber and mainsail reafed and ran on the reef at bout on[e] half mild [mile] from the beach and thumped heavy. Hove lumber over bord. Went off at 1 oclock. Went on and went ashore on the east bank at West Pass about one mild from same island. Water braking over at 4 P.M. Could see the men leave the vessel and land on St Vinsan island."

St. Vincent Island, mentioned in the earlier logbook citation as St Vinsan, lies to the northwest of St. George Island. Before the federal government acquired the island and made it part of the national wildlife refuge system, its private owners imported many exotic animals, including sambar deer and black buck from India, zebra and eland from Africa, and wild hogs. One eland bull, a type of large oxlike antelope, escaped and swam the short distance to the mainland, where some very surprised hunters killed it, not knowing what strange animal they had encountered.

Alexander Key's novel *Island Light* (Bobbs-Merrill, 1950) is about the Cape St. George Lighthouse. The novel tells the story of how difficult life on the island was for the keepers' families, especially when they did not get along with each other. It also dealt with the dangers of the job, for example in hanging perilously from the tower and trying to paint it, and the common belief on many such islands that pirates had buried treasure somewhere in its sands. The keeper pointed out in the story that many former seamen entered the lighthouse service because they knew the sea well and appreciated the importance of maintaining a light each night for mariners offshore. It is a good novel for learning more of the personal lives of a typical keeper's family on a remote island.

After much debate in the 1940s and early 1950s about the feasibility of cutting St. George Island in two in order to provide local fishermen a quick approach to the Gulf, workers dredged open Sikes Cut across St. George Island in 1954; named after U. S. Congressman Bob Sikes, the channel has greatly facilitated the time it takes local fishermen to get to the Gulf, but it may also have contributed to the increased salinity in the bay. In 1956, the U.S. Army Corps of Engineers built two jetties on the Gulf side near the lighthouse and redredged the canal to a depth of ten feet because it was beginning to close up. The debate continues as to whether Sikes Cut has been detrimental to the oyster harvest in the bay, but the fishermen who want the channel have won for the time being.

A 1961 fire destroyed a single-story wood frame dwelling at the lighthouse site, as well as a two-storied brick dwelling, a pumphouse, stable, storeroom, and generator building. In 1965, workers built a causeway and toll bridge to connect St. George Island with the mainland, but the lighthouse remains isolated on Little St. George Island.

How to get to the lighthouse

Go by boat to Cape St. George. A boat can be hired in Apalachicola for the run across the bay.

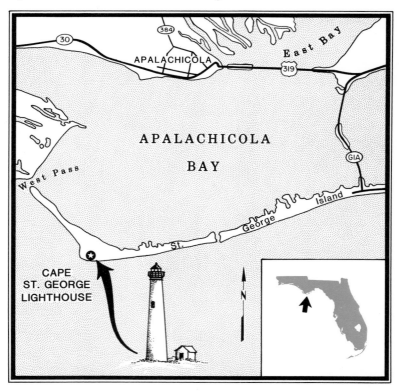

29

Cape San Blas Lighthouse

Ships passing along the Florida coast, east from the port of Panama City or west from the port of Apalachicola, had to contend with a dangerous shoal that extended five or six miles from Cape San Blas (pronounced "blass"). Spaniards named the cape for the martyred bishop of Sebaste in Armenia. That cape at the end of St. Joseph Peninsula or Spit is about 14 miles from Port St. Joe. According to geologists, 5,000 years ago the peninsula consisted of two barrier islands; approximately a thousand years ago the two islands joined at Eagle Harbor and at the mainland, forming St. Joseph Peninsula and Cape San Blas.

The dangerous shoal off the coast necessitated some type of navigational aid, despite the fact that the captain of one revenue cutter in 1838 considered the building of a lighthouse at Cape San Blas a useless expenditure. Local people pointed out that a high-enough light, one that could be seen 20 miles at sea, could help ships going from the Dry Tortugas near Key West to New Orleans. Engineers finally built the first lighthouse in 1847 at Cape San Blas, and it lasted four years. After a storm toppled it into the sea in 1851, Congress authorized a second one, which workers finished in 1856, just as the Great Storm of 1856 arrived to topple it. That storm was so severe that the waves washed the floor of the keeper's dwelling, eight feet above the ground and about 14 feet above ordinary tides.

The Lighthouse Board then built a third brick tower in 1859, but Confederate troops took it over at the start of the Civil War and burned everything in sight, including the keeper's home. By luck, the expensive prisms were mostly undamaged. The Confederates were attempting to foil attempts by Union forces to land on the shore and destroy the many salt works located there, works that provided the Confederates with the much-needed preservative.

After the war, authorities relighted the lighthouse on 23 July 1865; they built a new keeper's home in 1870, which allowed the

Cape San Blas Lighthouse

keeper to move out of the watch tower. At about that time, the encroaching Gulf was washing the base of the lighthouse and threatening to topple it into the sea, but it lasted another 12 years, finally collapsing in July 1882. Right before it collapsed, notices in newspapers warned mariners that the keeper could not monitor the light in the tower when the seas were rough, which was precisely one of the times that mariners needed a light. Two months later, a hurricane destroyed the keeper's house. Workers had used woven brush mattresses pinned down to the sand with small iron screwpiles, covered with sand and blocks of concrete, to try to stop the encroaching sea, but without success.

Realizing the futility of building a brick tower, authorities then built a movable iron skeleton tower, which was modeled after the one on Sanibel Island near Fort Myers. The ship bringing the tower sank, but the water was so shallow that workers salvaged the structure. While the new lighthouse was being built, engineers put a sixth-order fixed beacon on top of a 90-foot log on the shore to help mariners passing along the coast. Work on the structure was delayed by malarial sickness, which the long drought had brought on, but workers finally finished it in June 1885 and placed it 900 feet from the Gulf. By 1894, the water was again washing up around the tower, so authorities chose Black's Island in the bay as the fifth site for a lighthouse; after they finished the tower foundation and the keeper's house, they ran out of money and had to abandon the project. Giving up on the Black's Island site, authorities placed the new tower near its original site at the Cape. By 1918, because of much sand erosion, engineers had to move the tower 1,850 feet from the water.

In 1895, Charles Lupton was reassigned from the Seahorse Key Lighthouse near Cedar Key to the Cape San Blas Lighthouse. He and his family made the 180-mile trip by schooner, a trip that lasted eight full days because of a slight breeze. The Cape San Blas site was so isolated and far from other towns that a trip to the mainland was a large undertaking. Lupton used to go by mule and wagon to Apalachicola twice a year to buy supplies, making the 56-mile trip (28 miles each way) in three days: one day to go, one day for the mules to rest, and a third day to return.

Because St. Joseph Peninsula and Cape San Blas form a barrier structure in the Gulf, they attract thousands of migrating birds twice a year. In the fall, southbound warblers, vireos, and tanagers use the peninsula for a final staging area before making the long trip to Central and South America and the Caribbean islands. Birdwatchers arrive in October to see several species of hawks and falcons and the endangered peregrine falcon. In the spring, thousands of birds land on the peninsula and remain for several weeks before heading north. Such birds can cause much grief to a lighthouse keeper as they are attracted to the light at nighttime.

Tragedy struck the Cape San Blas Lighthouse in 1938 when an intruder killed assistant keeper E. W. Marler. On 16 March, Marler had left his house to work in his garden, and, when he did not return for the noon meal, his wife sent one of their four children to look for him. The little girl found her father lying in a pool of blood with a slashed wrist and fifteen stab wounds. At first, investigators thought he might have killed himself, but on further investigation they realized that he could not have done it. Authorities never did apprehend the murderer.

Today one can see the iron skeleton lighthouse tower and the two nearby two-storied, six-room frame dwellings used by the keepers. The lantern is 96 feet above the ground and 101 feet above sea level. Mariners can see the light 25 miles at sea as it flashes white every twenty seconds for one second. A radio beacon also transmits on 320 kilohertz. It may be hard to imagine that the sea, which seems to be quite a distance away, has caused so much damage over the years to the different lighthouses in the area. The cape has had more lighthouses than most other Florida sites, but the latest one seems distant enough from the sea, flexible enough for a quick move, and strong enough to withstand winds so that it should last for a long time.

How to get to the lighthouse

From Apalachicola or Port St. Joe take U.S. 98, then S.R. 30, then S.R. 30E to a U.S. radar station; 0.4 mile beyond the radar station, take the road that bears to the left. The lighthouse is 0.75 mile down on the right in the middle of some trees on government property.

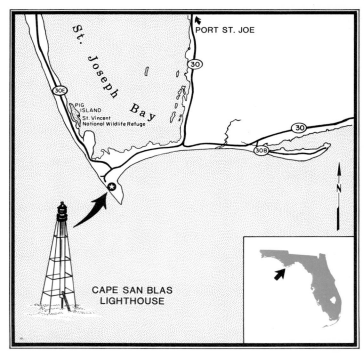

CAPE SAN BLAS
LIGHTHOUSE

30

St. Joseph Bay Lighthouse

When the territory of Florida was trying to decide in the late 1830s whether to try to become a state, the town of St. Joseph near Apalachicola saw an opportunity to promote itself. Experiencing a rapid rise that few other Florida towns could match, leaders in the small boomtown managed to lure the state's first constitutional convention in late 1838 to draft Florida's first constitution. To better its economic position, the town tried to build two railroads to divert river traffic from its rival, Apalachicola, but it did not work.

St. Joseph was situated on St. Joseph Bay, protected from the open Gulf of Mexico by St. Joseph Peninsula. The bay, oval in shape, has one opening to the Gulf: a narrow passage at the northern tip of the peninsula. In order to mark the entrance to St. Joseph Bay and to help ships avoid the shoals off Mexico Beach, the government first built a lighthouse on St. Joseph Peninsula at the entrance to the bay in 1838; the height of the tower from base to the fixed light was 50 feet. The outlook for the town of St. Joseph seemed promising until, in 1841, a ship came in with yellow fever on board; the ensuing epidemic killed off the inhabitants of the town, and a hurricane destroyed its houses. The town never recovered from those double blows, and the lighthouse was discontinued in 1847 in favor of the Cape San Blas Lighthouse. The St. Joseph Lighthouse seems to have been washed away in 1851.

From time to time, the Lighthouse Board recommended that the St. Joseph Light be reactivated, especially as more and more fishermen used the bay. The area around St. Joseph Peninsula was a dangerous site, as evidenced by the loss of vessels, for example Pensacola's *W. J. Keyser,* a tug which sank in a storm in 1898.

That same year Congress finally appropriated the necessary funds, but the Lighthouse Board decided to place the new structure on the mainland instead of on St. Joseph Peninsula. Built at

St. Joseph Bay Lighthouse

Beacon Hill, it was officially called the St. Joseph Light Range Station and unofficially the Beacon Hill Light or the St. Joseph Bay Lighthouse. Unlike most Florida lighthouses, that one enabled the keeper and his family to live in the light structure rather than in a separate building. In 1902, workers completed the building and a 245-foot wharf that was six feet wide.

In an interview in the summer of 1988, I. C. Lupton, the son of keeper Charles Lupton, told how isolated it was there in the early part of this century, with few visitors to bring in news from the outside world. The family eagerly welcomed travelers passing through, even the occasional tramp who liked to spend a warm night in the barn behind the range station. The surrounding countryside consisted of pine forests, cypress swamps, and marshes full of wildflowers. The Gulf side was lined with miles of white beaches. The keeper and his family would occasionally hitch up their horse and wagon and go for supplies to the only community in the area, Farmdale, which lay at the eastern end of where Tyndall Air Force Base is today. About the only business in the area was a little turpentining.

During the summer many more people vacationed in the

122

area, especially from Alabama and Georgia; that is how nearby Mexico Beach got started. The lighthouse family was quite self-sufficient, having a garden and some cows and the means to hunt and fish. For education, Mr. Lupton arranged with Jim McNeil of Indian Pass about 15 miles away to have his daughter, Lillian McNeil, go to Beacon Hill and tutor the Lupton children for $15 a month plus board. For a few years during World War I she would go each Sunday and stay till Friday, doing that for a few months each winter. I. C. Lupton also mentioned how everyone was very careful around the house since the doctor was too far away for easy visits.

The keeper's house at Beacon Hill consisted of three bedrooms, a living room, and a kitchen/dining room. A watch-room over the center of the building had a third-order iron lantern over it with a lens that showed a fixed white light. The building was raised off the ground about 10 or 12 feet on great big brick pillars. Under the building were storerooms for paints and supplies and a large cistern that held rainwater until workers drilled a well. Later, the ground-level area was walled in and converted into soldiers' quarters and a stable; troops used to patrol the coast during World War II looking for enemy invaders.

On the top of the house was a light, 96 feet above sea level that could be seen 13 miles out at sea. The keeper would light the three-wick apparatus at 9 P.M., go to bed, rise at daylight, and put the lights out. He also had to record the daily weather in his ledger each evening.

Heavy, diamond-shaped windows lined the lighthouse room, which the keeper would reach by climbing a narrow, circular stairway. A storeroom near the staircase held the necessary supplies. A large iron door led outside to a narrow walkway. The keeper and his family had to keep the brass on the light polished by using the buckskin provided by the government.

The keeper also had to light the beach beacon near the shore, 600 feet from the house down a narrow red-brick walkway. Ships entering St. Joseph Bay lined up the beach beacon, the light at the top of the house, and a sea buoy out in the bay in order to come through the pass.

When asked about any shipwrecks, I. C. Lupton recalled one that came ashore during Prohibition. During a big storm, a ship got stranded offshore and, to lighten their load, the sailors unloaded a great quantity of illegal whiskey. Mr. Lupton told the men that they had set the whiskey on government property. He told them that if they had just gone down the beach a little ways, he wouldn't have bothered them, but, because they had unknowingly unloaded it on government property, he had to report them to the authorities. Before said authorities could remove the contraband liquor, news of the incident spread throughout the community, and people hurried down to the beach to take the whiskey for themselves.

When the U.S. government discontinued the St. Joseph Light Range Station, the old building was abandoned to the elements and was eventually moved to the Overstreet Highway for use as a barn. In 1979, Danny Raffield of Port St. Joe moved it to Simmons Bayou and converted it into a private home.

How to get to the lighthouse

From Port St. Joe, the restored building is off U.S. 98 on the way to Indian Pass, just west of a fish camp. In Beacon Hill, 9.9 miles west of Port St. Joe and west of Beacon Road, a steel tower can be seen along the highway about 100 yards from where the Beacon Hill Lighthouse stood.

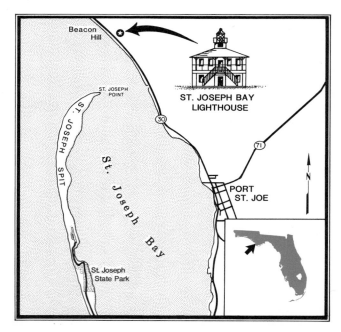

31

Pensacola Lighthouse

Pensacola is the second oldest city in Florida. Unlike the oldest city, St. Augustine, which has capitalized on its antiquity and history, Pensacola has been slow to exploit its historic ties to Spain, France, and England. Only in the last decade or so has it begun to celebrate its past with pageants and activities to draw in the tourist, but the downtown area around Seville Square and the restored houses and exhibits still have a tastefulness about them.

The city also differed from other Florida settlements in that it looked west for its development and identity, especially to New Orleans and the French influence. The name of the city comes from an Indian tribe, the Pansfalaya or "long-haired people," a name referring to the way the men and women wore their hair.

The Spanish explorer Don Tristán de Luna established a colony in the area in 1559, six years before the founding of St. Augustine, but in 1561 the settlers abandoned the site. The Spanish established a more permanent site in 1698. In 1821, Andrew Jackson officially accepted the transfer of the Floridas to the United States from Spain there, and Pensacola became the first capital of the Territory of West Florida. Five nations have con- trolled the area: Spain, three times (1698–1719, 1723–63, 1783–1821); France (1719–23); England (1763–83); the Con- federate States of America (1861–62); and the United States, twice (1821–61, 1862–present). Such drastic shifts might give an identity crisis to some cities, but Pensacola has adapted well.

Soon after the United States acquired Florida from Spain, the Florida Legislative Council asked President James Monroe to authorize the construction of a federal naval depot at Pensacola. Washington, interested in the Caribbean area, saw the need for a lighthouse and the expediency of using the port there, the deepest port on the northern Gulf of Mexico, 21 feet at the entrance and 36 feet in the harbor.

In early 1823, before they could build a lighthouse, authorities had the customs collector at New Orleans send a lightship from

Pensacola Lighthouse

the mouth of the Mississippi River to Pensacola. That vessel, the *Aurora Borealis,* was at its new post by 22 June, but problems associated with the lightship pointed up the inadequacies of moored vessels compared to land-based towers. In order to protect the vessel from rough seas, the captain had to anchor her near Santa Rosa Island, but that diminished her usefulness because ships at sea either could not see her or could not steer directly for her.

In 1824, the U.S. government designated Pensacola the site of a navy yard. Workers built a 40-foot lighthouse on a 40-foot bluff at the south entrance to Pensacola Bay, making the light 80 feet above sea level, and lighted it in 1825, making it the first

126

lighthouse built by the U.S. government on Florida's Gulf coast. The tower used the Argand lamp with parabolic reflectors, which were soon out of date.

Jeremiah Ingraham served as the first keeper from 1825 until his death in 1840, at which time his wife took over his duties until 1855. In 1837, an inspector recommended that the tower be moved to higher ground, partly because pine trees nearby and on Santa Rosa Island obscured its light, but nothing was done. In 1851, another investigator found that the light was little better than a harbor light. The changing of Mobile Light, 40 miles away, from a stationary light to a revolving one similar to the Pensacola Lighthouse confused mariners.

After more study, in 1858 engineers erected a new tower on the north side of the bay's entrance. First lighted on 1 January 1859, the first-order revolving light finally gave to the harbor the necessary beacon. During the Civil War, Confederate soldiers shot out the light, which remained out of operation until 1863, when a fourth-order lens relighted the tower. That lens was replaced in 1869 by a first-order lens.

During the Civil War the tower was completely white, but today the lower third is white, and the upper part is black. In 1914, the federal government established in Pensacola its first training base for naval aviators. Now known as the cradle of naval aviation, the base has from time to time suggested that the tall lighthouse is a hazard to low-flying airplanes, but local sentiment has prevented its razing. Aircraft pilots now use the tower as a checkpoint.

The Coast Guard has been in charge of the tower since 1939. In 1960, workers sandblasted the exterior of the tower, cleaned the mortar joints, and repainted the rusty metal plates at the top. In 1974, the buildings went on the National Register of Historic Places. Today the lighthouse has four 1,000-watt bulbs in the light, but only one is in operation at a time. When a bulb burns out, another automatically flips into place. The powerful lens magnifies the light to 40,000 candlepower, which is visible 27 miles at sea. Originally, the keepers had to wind up the lighting mechanism every four hours, but now electricity takes care of that tedious work.

Finally there is the Pensacola Lighthouse Orchestra of Uppsala, Sweden. In 1979, a Swedish musician wrote to the mayor of Pensacola to say that his band had decided to name themselves the Pensacola Lighthouse Orchestra and wanted to know if Pensa-

cola really had a lighthouse. They chose the name Pensacola because of its Spanish tone and because they wanted the name of an
American city to match the music they played. The mayor wrote
back saying that the city did have a lighthouse and that he would
make the members of the band honorary citizens of the city. The
band then decided to use the lighthouse as the logo on its folders
and music stands. If nothing else, one Florida lighthouse should
become better known in Europe.

How to get to the lighthouse

From I-95 take U.S. 29 (Pensacola Boulevard) to Palafax Highway
to Pace Boulevard to Barrancas Avenue to S.R. 295, which leads to the
U.S. Naval Air Station. The guard at the entrance to the Air Station will
give directions to those wanting to visit the lighthouse. The nearby
Naval Aviation Museum, which is open to visitors, gives a good overall
history of the base, including the lighthouse.

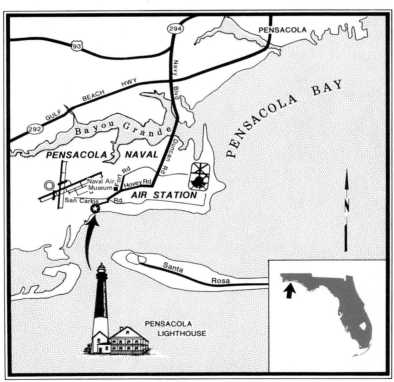

Adams, John Quincy, 73
"After the Storm," 75
Ais Indians, 29
Allen, William, 53
Alligator, 53
Alligator Reef Lighthouse,
  53–56, 67, 88
Amelia Island, 5, 21
Amelia Island Lighthouse, 5–8,
  10
American Shoal Lighthouse,
  61–64, 68
American Shoals, 61
Anastasia Island, 21, 23, 24, 46
Anclote Key, 97, 100
Anclote Key Lighthouse, 97–100
Anclote River, 97
Andreu, John, 21
Apalachee Bay, 105, 107
Apalachicola, 111, 113, 116,
  117, 119–21
Apalachicola Bay, 113
Apalachicola River, 110, 113
Atlantic to Gulf railroad, 103
Audubon Society, 36
Aurora Borealis, 126

Babcock, Orville, 27
Bahama Banks, 38
Banana River, 30
Barnegat Lighthouse, 3
Battle of Dunn Lawton, 27

Battle of Gettysburg, 33, 103
Beacon Hill Light, 122, 123
Bernard, Barbier, 7
Bethel, William, 71
Biddles, 90
Big Diamond, 39
Bill Baggs Cape Florida State
  Recreation Area, 43
Biscayne Bay, 37, 45, 53
Biscayne National Monument,
  47–48
Bloxham, W. D., 81
Boca Grande, 85–92
Boca Grande Causeway, 91
Boca Grande Lighthouse, 89–92
Boca Grande Pass, 85–87
Booth, John Wilkes, 75
Bowles, William Augustus, 102,
  105
Brightman, Latham, 65
Broward County, 37
Browne, Jefferson, 47
Brunswick, 14
Bureau of Lighthouses, 3
Burnham, Mills, 29–31, 39

Cabo de las Corrientes, 29
Caladese State Park, 97
Calusa Indians, 49
Canal de Yucatan, 79
Cape Canaveral Lighthouse,
  29–32, 39

Index

Cape Florida, 43, 69
Cape Florida Lighthouse, 2, 34, 41–44, 47, 48, 51
Cape Hatteras Lighthouse, 21
Cape Kennedy, 31
Cape St. George Lighthouse, 109, 113–16
Cape San Blas Lighthouse, 17, 97, 117–21
Carabelle, 109–13
Carabelle River, 110
Carysfort Reef Lighthouse, 49–52, 55, 57, 67
Carysfort Reef lightship, 51
Casa Ybel, 81
Castillo de San Marcos, 23
Cedar Key, 5, 101–4, 119
Charlotte County, 85
Charlotte Harbor, 85, 89
Coacoochee, 27
Commodore, 25
Cooley, William, 41
Cooper, James Fenimore, 23, 74
Coquina, 22, 23
Corps of Engineers, 43, 73, 99, 115
Cosgrove, P. O., 74
Crane, Stephen, 25
Crooked River Lighthouse, 17, 109–12
Cross-Florida Barge Canal, 99
Cuban Revolution, 25

Dade, Francis L., 95
Daytona Beach, 25, 27, 29
Deadman's Key, 101
Dean, Love, 63
de León, Ponce, 29, 73, 93
de Luna, Don Tristán, 125
DeMeritt, William, 71
de Narváez, Panfilo, 93
De Soto, Hernando, 93

Dickinson, Jonathan, 33
Dog Island, 109, 110, 113
Drake, Francis, 21
Drexels, 90
Dry Tortugas, 45, 68, 73, 77, 117
Dry Tortugas Lighthouse, 77–80
Dubose, James, 41
DuPonts, 90

Egmont Key Lighthouse, 17, 82, 91, 93–96
Eichhoff, Michael, 59

Fernandina Beach, 5
Flagler, Henry, 37, 71
Flaherty, John, 65
Flaherty, William, 73
Florida Bay, 45, 53
"Florida Beach, The," 23
Florida East Coast Railroad, 37
Florida Keys, 45
Florida Reef, 1, 37, 46, 49, 55
Florida Straits, 63, 65, 79
Fort Dade, 95
Fort George Island, 10
Fort Jefferson, 73–77, 80
Fort Lauderdale, 37
Fort San Marcos de Apalache, 105, 107
Fowey Rocks Lighthouse, 43, 45–48, 55, 61, 67
Franklin County, 109, 110
Fresnel, Augustin, 17

Garden Key, 73
Garden Key Lighthouse, 73–76
Gaspar, Friar, 85
Gaspar, José, 85
Gasparilla Inn, 90
Gasparilla Island, 85–89, 92
Gasparilla Pass, 85
Gauld, George, 93

Index

Gomez, John, 85
Gorrie, John, 113
Great Freeze of 1894–95, 37
Great St. Louis Exposition, 38
Great Storm of 1856, 117
Greshams, 106–7
Gulf of Mexico, 1, 79, 121, 125
Gulf Stream, 1, 37, 45, 48, 53, 59, 63, 65, 67, 79

Halifax River, 25, 27, 28
Hall, Carrie, 110
Hamilton, James, 37
Hardee, Cary, 107
Hemingway, Ernest, 61, 67, 75, 77
Hillsboro, 39
Hillsboro Inlet Lighthouse, 37–40
Hillsboro Point, 37
HMS *Carysford,* 49
HMS *Fowey,* 46
Honda Bay, 68
Housman, Jacob, 53
Hurricane Betsy (1965), 67
Hurricane Donna (1960), 67
Hurricane (Labor Day, 1935), 55, 67, 71

Indian Key, 53
Indian River, 25, 33
Ingraham, Jeremiah, 127
Intracoastal Waterway, 9, 37
Island Light, 115

Jackson, Andrew, 105, 125
Jacksonville, 9, 13
Jacksonville Beach, 3, 19
Jack Tier, 74
J. N. "Ding" Darling National Wildlife Refuge, 83
Johnson, Captain, 51
Johnson, Charles, 67

Johnson, John, 82
Johnson, President Lyndon, 31
Jupiter Inlet Lighthouse, 33–38
Jupiter Island, 35

Key, Alexander, 115
Key Biscayne, 41, 43, 51
Key Largo, 49, 50, 52, 53, 69
Key West, 34, 43, 45, 47, 50, 51, 61, 63, 65–74, 76, 78–82, 93
Key West Art and Historical Society, 71
Key West Lighthouse, 68–72
Knight, James M., 31
Knight, Thomas, 39

Labrador Current, 1
Lafitte, Jean, 101
Lake Elsmere, 14
Las Tortugas, 73
Latham, Amos, 7
LeBlanc, Pierre, 101, 102
Lee County, 87
Lee, Robert E., 33, 93
Lenape, 14
Lewis, Winslow, 26
Lighthouse Automation and Modernization Program (LAMP), 19
Lighthouse Board, 3, 31, 33, 37, 43, 61, 81, 109, 117, 121
Lighthouse Museum, 3
Lighthouse Point, 39
Lighthouse Service, 71, 83, 86
Light List, 27
Lightship, 11, 13–15, 50, 51, 126
Little Conch Reef, 55
Little Cumberland Island, 11
Little St. George Island, 114, 116
Loggerhead, 68, 77
Loggerhead Key, 79
Los Mosquitos, 25

Index

Loxahatchee River, 33
Lupton, Charles, 119, 122
Lupton, I.C., 122, 123

Mabrity, Barbara, 70
Mabrity, Michael, 70
McNeil, Jim, 123
McNeil, Lillian, 123
Maine, 74
Mallory, Stephen, 29
Mangrove, 74
Mansfield, Mike, 87
Marathon, 57, 59
Marquesas, 68
Mayport, 9, 11, 12, 14, 15, 21
Mayport Lighthouse, 11
Mayport Naval Air Station, 9, 11, 12, 16, 20
Meade, George, 33, 57, 103
Mexico Beach, 121, 123
Miami, 37
Mission San Juan del Puerto , 9
Mobile Light, 127
Molasses Key, 57
Money Key, 57
Monroe, James, 53, 125
Monroe, Kirk, 67
Monroe County, 47, 67
Morgan, Harry, 67
Mosquito County, 25
Mosquito Inlet Lighthouse, 25
Mosquito River, 25
Mudd, Samuel, 74, 75

Nassau Sound, 5
National Archives, 3
National Register of Historic Places, 11, 27, 43, 83, 87, 95, 127
National Weather Service, 19, 78
Nature Conservancy, 36
New Smyrna, 25

New Smyrna Beach, 28
Ochlockonee River, 110
O'Hagan, Thomas J., 7
Oklawaha River, 99
"Open Boat, The," 25
Orange County, 25
Ormond, James III, 27
Overseas Highway, 61, 71
Overseas Railroad, 47, 71

Palm Land, 91
Panther Key, 85
Peace River, 86, 89
Pensacola, 17, 69, 125–28
Pensacola Bay, 127
Pensacola Lighthouse, 125–28
Pensacola Lighthouse Orchestra, 127, 128
Perceval, John, 93
Perrine, Henry, 53, 54
Perry, Matthew, 69
Pierce, Charles W., 35
Pleasonton, Stephen, 21
Pompano Beach, 37, 39
Ponce, Antonio, 27
Ponce de Leon Inlet Lighthouse, 17, 21, 25–28, 46, 88
Ponce Inlet, 27
Port Boca Grande, 87
Port Boca Grande Lighthouse, 85–89, 92
Port Canaveral, 31
Porter, David, 53
Port St. Joe, 3, 117, 120, 124
Prohibition, 27
Punta Gorda, 89
Punta Rassa, 81

Quarterman, George, 31

Rebecca's Shoal, 68, 75
Red Badge of Courage, The , 25

Index

Reef Lights, 63
Reike, Rudolph, 57
Relief, 15
Ribault, Jean, 9
Richardson, Dudley, 82
Rickleth, John, 57
Ringling, Mable, 107
Río Carrabelle, 110
Río de Corrientes, 9
Roberts, E. W., 107
Roosevelt, Franklin, 75
Rutland, Clarence, 82

Saddlebunch Keys, 61
Sagamore, 34
St. Augustine Lighthouse, 11,
    21–24
St. George Island, 110, 113,
    115, 116
St. George Sound, 113
St. Johns Lightship, 13–16
St. Johns Light Station, 17–20
St. Johns River, 9, 10, 99
St. Johns River Lighthouse,
    9–13, 17
St. Joseph, 121
St. Joseph Bay Lighthouse,
    121–24
St. Joseph Peninsula, 117, 119,
    121
St. Marks Lighthouse, 17, 88,
    105–8
St. Marks National Wildlife
    Refuge, 107, 108
St. Marks River, 105
St. Marys River, 5
St. Vincent Island, 115
Sand Key Lighthouse, 51, 57,
    61, 65–69
Sanibel, 17, 83, 84, 93
Sanibel Causeway, 81, 84
Sanibel Island Lighthouse,
    81–84, 119
Screw-pile lighthouses, 17, 65, 66,
    88
Seaboard Coast Line, 89, 91
Seabrook, Charles, 35
Seahorse Key Lighthouse, 99,
    101–4, 119
Sea Island, 5
Second Seminole War, 41, 102
Seminole Indian Wars, 27, 105–6
Seven-Mile Bridge, 57, 59
Shanahan, Eugene, 82
Shanahan, Henry, 82
Sikes, Bob, 115
Sikes Cut, 115
Silver Star, 91
Smith, Alexander, 57
Smith, Edmund Kirby, 113
Smith, Jarrell, 27
Snake Key, 101
Sombrero Key Lighthouse, 55,
    57–61, 68
Southwest Channel, 65
Straits of Florida, 45
Submarines, 24, 31, 59, 99, 111
Sugarloaf Key, 64
Suwannee River, 101
Sydam, 7
Sykes, Sir Tatton, 29
Sykes Creek, 29

Ten Thousand Islands, 85
Territory of Florida, 9
Territory of West Florida, 125
Thames River, 13
Thompson, John, 41–43
To Have and Have Not, 61, 67, 77
Tortugas, 69, 75
Treasury Department, 2
Trotter, Bill, 3

University of Florida, 103

Index

U.S. Fish and Wildlife Service, 95
Volusia County, 25

Waccasassa River, 101
Wellington, Captain, 51
Whalton, John, 50, 51
Whitehead Point, 70
Wickies, 17
Wildcat, 27
Williams, James, 111

Williams, William H., 26
Wilson, Henry, 31
Wilson, William, 103
Withlacoochee River, 99
W. J. Keyser, 121
Woolson, Constance Fenimore, 23
Wreckers, 1, 49, 51, 53, 55, 62, 69

Yulee, David, 103